EXISTENTIAL
PSYCHOANALYSIS

JEAN-PAUL SARTRE

EXISTENTIAL PSYCHOANALYSIS

Translated by
Hazel E. Barnes

Introduction by
Rollo May

A GATEWAY EDITION
REGNERY GATEWAY
Washington, D.C.

TABLE OF CONTENTS

TRANSLATOR'S PREFACE

THE TWO essays here presented are taken from Jean-Paul Sartre's *Being and Nothingness (L'être et le néant)*. "Bad Faith" is the second chapter of Part One. "Existential Psychoanalysis" is the second chapter of Part Four. In this volume I have reversed their relative position, for "Bad Faith" in actuality contains criticism and in a sense the specific application of ideas more fully developed in the other essay. Both essays contain references to other sections of *Being and Nothingness*. I have not deleted these since I feel that they may be useful for the reader who wishes either to consult the original or to wait for the complete translation on which I am now working.

I have included here an introduction, the intent of which is to furnish such information as will be helpful to readers who have not seen Sartre's original volume.

I should like to express sincere appreciation to Professor Gardner Williams, to Professor Robert S. Hartman, and to Professor Fritz Kaufmann for helpful suggestions. In particular I wish to thank Dr. Robert O. Lehnert and Miss Doris J. Schwalbe, both of whom spent many hours reading the work with me and offering valuable criticism.

HAZEL E. BARNES

EXISTENTIAL
PSYCHOANALYSIS

INTRODUCTION

by Rollo May

WHEN THE publishers asked me to write the introduction to this book, I hesitated because, as I remarked to them, I have two contrasting beliefs with respect to the work of Sartre. One is that his thought needs to be taken with genuine seriousness and is one of the unquestionably important contributions to modern Western man's interpretation of himself in philosophy, psychology, and literature. My other belief is that some of Sartre's underlying principles are basically mistaken. The publishers answered—and I could only agree with the wisdom of their argument—that an Introduction taking into account both these viewpoints was exactly the most constructive and fruitful way for Sartre to be presented to college students and other thoughtful modern people.

To appreciate Sartre's contribution we must of course first dissociate him from the superficial interpretations of his ideas by the extremists of the Café deux Magots and the left bank of the Seine and the Hudson. True,

Sartre himself has invited such misinterpretations with such superficially rash statements as that which ends Chapter III of this book, "Man is a useless passion." But behind the nihilistic implications of such a statement, there lies Sartre's passionate and perdurable insistence that man is not an object to be *used* by God or a higher intelligence, or manipulated by the juggernaut of modern industrialism, or fashioned into a mechanical passive consumer by mass communication.

Nor is man to be *used* by means of his own manipulation of himself as a psychological machine to be "adjusted," or moulded by Norman Vincent Peale's "positive thinking" into an organization man to win success on Madison Avenue. Man is not an object to be forced into the "role demanded by modern society—to be *only* a waiter or a conductor or a mother, *only* an employer or a worker," as Miss Hazel Barnes writes in her introduction to her translation of Sartre.[1] She goes on rightly to say, "To my mind this aspect of Sartre's existentialism is one of his most positive and most important contributions— the attempt to make contemporary man look for himself again and refuse to be absorbed in a role on the stage of a puppet theater."

[1] The chapters on Sartre's psychology, entitled "A Psychology of Freedom," in Hazel Barnes' *The Literature of Possibility* (Lincoln: University of Nebraska Press, 1959) are to be recommended.

All through this book the reader will find, by the same token, Sartre's sharp attacks on the modern psychology which sees man as an object for conditioning, or holds that "the individual is only the intersection of universal schemata." (p. 22) Sartre writes: if we "consider man as capable of being analyzed and reduced to original data, to determined drives (or 'desires'), supported by the subject as properties of an object," we may indeed end up with an imposing system of substances which we may then call mechanisms or dynamisms or patterns. But we find ourselves up against a dilemma. Our human being has become "a sort of indeterminate clay which would have to receive (the desires) passively—or he would be reduced to a simple bundle of these irreducible drives or tendencies. In either case the *man* disappears; we can no longer find 'the one' to whom this or that experience has happened." [2]

Lest any readers feel that this issue of freedom and choice is a "straw man," or one of those theoretical problems the Europeans delight in coming up with, let me quote the following paragraph from a recent paper by Dr. Carl Rogers of the Departments of Psychology and Psychiatry at the University of Wisconsin:

[2] Jean-Paul Sartre, *Being and Nothingness*, trans. by Hazel Barnes (1956), p. 561.

Along with the development of technology has gone an underlying philosophy of rigid determinism in the psychological sciences which can perhaps best be illustrated by a brief exchange which I had with Prof. B. F. Skinner of Harvard at a recent conference. A paper given by Dr. Skinner led me to direct these remarks to him. "From what I understood Dr. Skinner to say, it is his understanding that though he might have thought he chose to come to this meeting, might have thought he had a purpose in giving his speech, such thoughts are really illusory. He actually made certain marks on paper and emitted certain sounds here simply because his genetic make-up and his past environment had operantly conditioned his behavior in such a way that it was rewarding to make these sounds, and that he as a person doesn't enter into this. In fact if I get his thinking correctly, from his strictly scientific point of view, he, as a person, doesn't exist." In his reply Dr. Skinner said that he would not go into the question of whether he had any choice in the matter (presumably because the whole issue is illusory) but stated, "I do accept your characterization of my own presence here." I do not need to labor the point that for Dr. Skinner the concept of "learning to be free" would be quite meaningless.[3]

This illustration—which could be multiplied many times over in almost every con-

---

[3] From the mimeographed transcription of the Conference on Evolutionary Theory and Human Progress: Conference C, The Individual and the Design of Culture, Dec. 2-4, 1960, pages 15-16, 79.

temporary discussion at conferences—shows
that nothing is more critical and timely than
just this problem of freedom and choice in
American psychology. Dr. Skinner represents
exactly the viewpoint which Sartre is attacking. And whereas there are many differences
between Sartre and Rogers, Sartre's analysis
of this issue would emphatically be on the
side of Rogers.

Sartre thus presents us with the most em-
phatic statement of human freedom and individual responsibility. "I *am* my choices," he
repeats again and again in various forms. In
his seeing freedom as the central and unique
potentiality that constitutes man as the
human being, Sartre gives the most extreme
statement of modern existentialism. In his
dramas he asserts this principle continually
and powerfully: Orestes, the chief character
in *The Flies,* shouts out against a manipu-
lating and dilettante Zeus, "I *am* my freedom!" Undaunted by Zeus' reminders of the
great despair and anxiety which dog the steps
of the free man, Orestes cries, "Human life
begins on the far side of despair!"

The Sartrean man, it is true, becomes a
solitary individual creature standing on the
basis of his defiance alone against God and
society. The philosophical basis of this principle is given in Sartre's famous statement,
"Freedom is existence, and in it existence pre-

cedes essence." That is to say, there would
be no *essences*—no truth, no structure in
reality, no logical forms, no *logos*, no God
nor any morality—except as man in affirming
his freedom makes these truths.

This brings us to what, in my judgment,
is the fundamental criticism of Sartre's
thought. I wish to present this criticism in
the words of Paul Tillich, who sees with
balanced wisdom the meaning of the modern
existential movement and also Sartre's position in it:

In contrast to the situation in the last three
years after the second World War, when most
people identified existentialism with Sartre,
it is now common knowledge in this country
that existentialism in the western intellectual
history starts with Pascal in the 17th century,
has an underground history in the 18th century, a revolutionary history in the 19th century and an astonishing victory in the 20th
century. Existentialism has become the style
of our period in all realms of life. Even the
analytic philosophers pay tribute to it by with-
drawing into formal problems and leaving
the field of material problems to the existen-
tialists in art and literature.

There are, however, only rare moments in
this monumental development in which an
almost pure existentialism has been reached.
An example is Sartre's doctrine of man. I
refer to a sentence in which the whole problem of essentialism and existentialism comes
into the open, his famous statement that

man's essence is his existence. The meaning of this sentence is that man is a being of whom no essence can be affirmed, for such an essence would introduce a permanent element, contradictory to man's power of transforming himself indefinitely. According to Sartre, man is what he acts to be.

But if we ask whether his statement has not, against its intention, given an assertion about man's essential nature, we must say, certainly, it has. Man's particular nature is his power to create himself. And if the further question is raised of how such a power is possible and how it must be structured, we need a fully developed essentialist doctrine in order to answer; we must know about his body and his mind, in short, about those questions which for millennia have been discussed in essentialist terms.

Only on the basis of an essentialist doctrine of freedom does Sartre's statement have any meaning. Neither in theology nor in philosophy can existentialism live by itself. It can only exist as a contrasting element within an essentialist framework.[4]

In other words, you cannot have freedom or a free individual without some structure in which (or in the case of defiance, *against* which) the individual acts. Freedom and structure imply each other. In my judgment, Sartre presupposes much more of the humanistic tradition of Western thought, and even

[4] Tillich, Paul. "Existentialism and Psychotherapy," *Review of Existential Psychology and Psychiatry*, Vol. I, No. 1, p. 9.

much more of the Hebrew-Christian concept of the significance and worth of the person, than he seems to be aware of or explicitly states. He also presupposes the Hebrew-Christian belief in the moral meaning of history. The prophets Amos and Isaiah, for example, cry out against wickedness on the basis of principles of justice to which even God was held accountable. Sartre presupposes similar moral principles in his defiance. There is an assumption all through Sartre—owing much to Descartes, inherent in French rationalism, given added conviction by the passionate beliefs of Kierkegaard and Nietzsche—that there is a meaningful structure in life and even in Western bourgeois society to make it possible that such a one as Sartre can fight so powerfully *against* them. To set out to become an Anti-Christ, as did Nietzsche, means to presuppose a Christ.

The same thing certainly can be said about Sartre's approach to psychoanalysis. In this volume, he presupposes Freud in order to fight tellingly against him. The fact that psychoanalysis is possible at all, that man can overcome psychological problems and that one person (the analyst) can help another (the so-called patient) presupposes a meaningful structure in the human psyche, whether this structure is revealed in dreams, in slips of tongue, in memories of childhood history, in neurotic symptoms, or what not. This structure Freud tried to describe and then to systematize. That there are fundamental errors in the system which was the outcome of Freud's endeavor is clear. And I believe Sartre has succeeded in this book in piercing with his sharp and incisive scalpel a number of these errors. But he could not have done so except that he presupposed Freud's essentialist systematic endeavor to start with.

One place where Sartre presupposes Freud too much is in the title of this book. The name *Existential Psychoanalysis* suggests that Sartre will offer an alternative form of psychoanalysis. This he neither does nor seeks to do; indeed, he rightly acknowledges that a genuine existential psychoanalysis can not yet be formulated or written. This book, rather, makes basic criticisms of modern psychology, in general, and Freud's determinism, in particular, and gives Sartre's often brilliant analysis of these errors and his proposals for their correction. He indicates also in what direction an existential psychoanalysis might be developed. Sartre does all of this on the basis of his existential understanding of man, and his unshakeable conviction that the human being simply cannot be understood at all if we see in him only what our study of sub-human forms of life permits us to see, or if we reduce him to naturalistic or mechanical determinisms, or fragmentize him into separate instincts or sets of stimuli and response, or in any other way take away from the man we try to study his ultimate freedom and individual responsibility.

Let me now mention some of the central and, in my judgment, highly significant points Sartre develops in the following pages. I shall not try to do this logically or systematically, but rather in a way which I hope will indicate the nature and meaning of Sartre's contribution.

First, Sartre points out that the usual forms of "explaining" which dominate most psychology and psychoanalysis simply do not explain at all. Using the case of Flaubert and the question of how he became a writer, Sartre points out that Bourget's "explanation" in terms of general emotional patterns and Flaubert's alleged need to escape into the less violent forms of expression, into writing, covers up the very thing we need to understand. Also such "explanations" estrange us from the person; we lose Flaubert.

The Freudian mechanisms like "projection," "introjection," "transference" also don't explain, since you never can leap from a general abstract law to a unique particular person. As many of us discover in psychoanalysis, the critical problem is always to know whether the general law can be *applied* to this particular person at this given moment in his history. This is the Achilles heel of all general laws used to explain individual human beings, and is generally blithely skipped over in our too-simplified and too hasty beliefs in our special approach to science.

Nor will Sartre accept any "explanation" in terms of determinism by the past. Sartre is much too intelligent not to know that we all are subject to influences determining us at every point: we are determined by our birth in a particular family of particular cultural and economic status, determined by our bodies, by instinctual needs, by past emotional traumas, and so on ad infinitum. The only trouble is, he argues, none of these explanations ever tells us what we want to know —why a given person like Flaubert at a given point in history chooses to become a writer, and why does he affirm this decision in a hundred and one different ways and degrees at a hundred and one different times? The human reality, Sartre insists, "identifies and defines itself by the ends which it pursues," (p. 19) not by alleged hypothetical "causes" in the past.

Nor can you explain the "higher" by the "lower" in evolutionary terms. The crucial problem in understanding man is not what attributes he shares with the horse or dog or rat, but what constitutes him uniquely as man, the human being.

Further, we cannot explain the person by recourse to talk about environment. Sartre insists, and I think very rightly, that "the environment can act on the subject only to the exact extent that he comprehends it; that he transforms it into a situation." (p. 54) I take it that Sartre means by "comprehend" that the individual has a meaningful relationship with this "environment," which then becomes a situation. Many of us would (as Sartre would not) include elements of which the individual is unconscious in this meaningful relationship.

The psychoanalyst will not be able to apply one-to-one specific symbols, but will have "to rediscover at each step a symbol functioning in the particular case which he is considering." (p. 55) Sartre feels that the splitting up of the person into *ego* and *Id* does not help us. A person *is* his *Id* only as he adopts a passive attitude toward the so-called unconscious forces, urges, etc. which Freud posited therein.

In all these emphases Sartre ranges himself, like the other phenomenological psychologists, firmly on the side of the "understanding" psychologies rather than the "explanatory" ones. Nevertheless, existential psychology is not at all an anarchy or mysticism, but will have its principles.

Now to the positive side of Sartre's psychoanalysis. The central principle of existential psychoanalysis will not be *libido* or *will to power,* but the individual's *choice of being.* "The goal of existential psychoanalysis is to rediscover through these empirical, concrete projects the original mode in which each man has chosen his being." (p. 115) Again, "existential psychoanalysis is a method destined to bring to light, in a strictly objective form, the subjective choice by which each living person makes himself a person." (p. 58) If we admit the person is a totality, Sartre argues, we obviously cannot arrive at that totality by simply adding up diverse sums; we find it rather in a "choice of an intelligible character," for I am "nothing other than the choice of myself as a totality" (p. 34) in a concrete relationship with the world.

Behind all this, of course, lies Sartre's insistence on individual responsibility: "I *am* my choices." The reader will understand this better if he thinks of choices not simply as the "big" resolutions made at New Year's but as the specific, intentional way I relate to my world at this given moment. Indeed, even free association in psychoanalysis, if it is to be fruitful and viable, depends upon this giving of one's self to the process, a taking a chance; even recalling a repressed childhood memory requires such an intentional orientation to the world of which memory is a part. Though I think Sartre oversimplifies the problem of freedom, as I said above, I do not think we can avoid the searching cogency of his penetrating question, *Is not this choice the point par excellence to find revealed the totality of the human being?* As Paul Tillich remarks in another context, "Man becomes truly human only at the moment of decision."

Nor is this choice to be thought of as only on the level of consciousness, or consisting only of reflective, voluntary decisions. Sartre speaks of "spontaneous determinations of our being," and certainly he believes that in every choice the totality of the self—dreams, desires, tastes, powers, past experience and future hopes—is involved. Thus he would include some aspects of what the Freudians call the "unconscious" in his concept of choice.

The reader will also appreciate Sartre's discussion of "bad faith." The human being is distinguished by the fact that he can lie to himself, deceive himself. And to do this remarkable thing requires that I know on some level that *I* am the one lying to myself; otherwise I couldn't do it. "The lie is a behavior of transcendence," Sartre well remarks. (p. 157) To be in bad faith means to be guilty of not accepting one's self as a free person but as an object. Sartre holds that classical psychoanalysis takes away just this crucial center of responsibility for one's own self-deceit; classical psychoanalysis is based on the idea of a "lie without a liar." (p. 163)

Sartre is constrained to deny the existence of "the unconscious," since even in self-deceit I know I am the one deceiving myself; and the so-called "censor" which Freud postulated as standing at the door of the unconscious must also be conscious in order to know what to repress. In his denial of "the unconscious," Sartre is in the general line of the phenomenological psychologists and psychiatrists such as Goldstein, Binswanger and Boss.

So far as Sartre is attacking the "blank check," idea of the unconscious—the idea that we can explain anything by hypothesizing something down in the "unconscious" —I go along with him. But I believe he goes too far in his rejection. I have summed up this problem elsewhere, which I wish to quote here:

Now it must be admitted that the doctrine of the unconscious has played most notoriously into the contemporary tendencies to rationalize behavior, to avoid the reality of one's own existence, to act as though one were not himself doing the living. (The man in the street who has picked up the lingo says, "My unconscious did it.") The existential analysts are correct, in my judgment, in their criticism of the doctrine of the unconscious as a convenient blank check on which any causal explanation can be written or as a reservoir from which any deterministic theory can be drawn. But this is the "cellar" view of the unconscious, and objections to it should not be permitted to cancel out the great contribution that the historical meaning of the unconscious had in Freud's terms. Freud's great discovery and his perdurable contribution was to enlarge the sphere of the human personality beyond the immediate voluntarism and rationalism of Victorian man, to include in this enlarged sphere the "depths," that is, the irrational, the so-called repressed, hostile, and unacceptable urges, the forgotten aspects of experience, *ad infinitum.* The symbol for this vast enlarging of the domain of the personality was "the unconscious." The meaning of this discovery, namely the radical enlargement of being, is one of the great contributions of our day and must be retained.[5]

Finally, we should note Sartre's emphasis on *ontology*—the study of being, what constitutes man as man—as the necessary basis for psychoanalysis. Where ontology stops psychoanalysis beings; the "final discoveries of ontology are the first principles of psychoanalysis." (p. 61) Ontology is a difficult concept, but given right definition, I believe

[5] *Existence: A New Dimension in Psychiatry and Psychology,* ed. Rollo May, Ernest Angel, Henri Ellenberger (New York: Basic Books), Ch. II, p. 90-91. The two introductory chapters in this book, entitled "Origins of the Existential Movement in Psychology" and "Contributions of Existential Psychotherapy," are recommended to students wishing to pursue this development in its broader aspects. The volume, *Existence,* contains translations of writings of the practicing existential psychiatrists and psychologists in Europe.

Sartre's main idea here is entirely correct.[6]

We close this introduction by repeating Sartre's caution at the close of his chapter: his "psychoanalysis" is not supposed to be a worked-out new form of technical analysis. It is rather a direction and a quest, an endeavor to find principles for psycho-analysis which will do justice to what man genuinely *is,* the *human* being. Sartre himself believes in the great value of biographies for discovering these principles. Like Allport, Maslow, McKinnon, and Murray among the psychologists in this country, Sartre would study the "successfully adjusted actions of life," the writer's style, and other constructive creative aspects of behavior. These reveal—if we can understand them—the central meaning of human experience as much as and in some ways more than neurosis and psychosis.

[6] I have tried to present the ontological bases of psychotherapy in the paper, "Existential Bases of Psychotherapy," in *Existential Psychology,* issued in the Papers in Psychology Series (New York: Random House, 1961), edited by Rollo May.

I

EXISTENTIAL PSYCHOANALYSIS

IF IT IS true that human reality—as we have attempted to establish—identifies and defines itself by the ends which it pursues, then a study and classification of these ends becomes indispensable. In the preceding chapter we have considered the For-itself only from the point of view of its free project, which is the impulse by which it thrusts itself toward its end. We should now question this end itself, for it *forms a part* of absolute subjectivity and is, in fact, its transcendent, objective limit. This is what empirical psychology has hinted at by admitting that a particular man is defined by his desires. Here, however, we must be on our guard against two errors. First, the empirical psychologist while defining man by his desires, remains the victim of the illusion of substance. He views desire as being *in* man by virtue of being "contained" by his consciousness, and he believes that the meaning of the desire is inherent in the desire itself.

Thus he avoids everything which could evoke the idea of transcendence. But if I desire a house or a glass of water or a woman's body, how could this body, this glass, this piece of property reside in my desire, and how can my desire be anything but the consciousness of these objects as desirable? Let us beware then of considering these desires as little psychic entities dwelling in consciousness; they are consciousness itself in its original projective, transcendent structure, for consciousness is on principle consciousness of something.

The other error, which fundamentally is closely connected with the first, consists in considering psychological research as terminated as soon as the investigator has reached the concrete ensemble of empirical desires. Thus a man would be defined by the bundle of drives or tendencies which empirical observation could establish. Naturally the psychologist will not always limit himself to making up the *sum* of these tendencies; he will want to bring to light their relationships, their agreements and harmonies; he will try to present the ensemble of desires as a synthetic organization in which each desire acts on the others and influences them. A critic, for example, wishing to explain the "psychology" of Flaubert, will write that he "appeared in his early youth to know as his normal state, a continual exaltation resulting from the twofold feeling of his grandiose ambition and his invincible power . . . The effervescence of his young blood was *then* turned into literary passion as happens about the eighteenth year in precocious souls who find in the energy of style or the intensities of fiction some way of escaping from the need of violent action or of intense feeling, which torments them." [1]

In this passage there is an effort to reduce the complex personality of an adolescent to a few basic desires, as the chemist reduces compound bodies to merely a combination of simple bodies. The primitive data[2] will be grandiose ambition, the need of violent acttion and of intense feeling; these elements when they enter into combination, produce a permanent exaltation. Then—as Bourget remarks in a few words which we have not quoted—this exaltation nourished by numerous well chosen readings, is going to seek to delude itself by self-expression in fictions which will appease it symbolically and channel it. There in outline is the genesis of a literary "temperament."

Now in the first place such a psychological *analysis* proceeds from the postulate that an individual fact is produced by the intersection of abstract, universal laws. The fact to be ex-

---

[1] Paul Bourget: *Essai de Psychologie contemporaine*: G. Flaubert.
[2] French données. Literally "givens." Tr.

plained—which is here the literary disposition of the young Flaubert—is resolved into a
combination of *typical,* abstract desires such
as we meet in "the average adolescent." What
is concrete here is only their combination; in
themselves they are only possible patterns.
The abstract then is by hypothesis prior to
the concrete, and the concrete is only an organization of abstract qualities; the individual
is only the intersection of universal schemata.
But—aside from the logical absurdity of such
a postulate—we see clearly in the example
chosen, that it simply fails to explain what
makes the individuality of the project under
consideration. The fact that "the need to
feel intensely," a universal pattern, is dis-
guised and channeled into becoming the need
to write—this is not the *explanation* of the
"calling" of Flaubert; on the contrary, it is
what must be explained. Doubtless one could
invoke a thousand circumstances, known to
us and unknown, which have shaped this
need to feel into the need to act. But this is to
give up at the start all attempt to explain
and refers the question to the undiscover-
able.[3] In addition this method rejects the pure
individual, who has been banished from the
pure subjectivity of Flaubert into the external

[3] Since Flaubert's adolescence, so far as we can know it,
offers us nothing specific in this connection, we must suppose the action of imponderable facts which on principle
escape the critic.

circumstances of his life. Finally, Flaubert's correspondence proves that long before the "crisis of adolescence," from his earliest childhood, he was tormented by the need to write.

At each stage in the description just quoted, we meet with an hiatus. Why did ambition and the feeling of his power produce in Flaubert *exaltation* rather than tranquil waiting or gloomy impatience? Why did this exaltation express itself specifically in the need to act violently and feel intensely? Or rather why does this need make a sudden appearance by spontaneous generation at the end of the paragraph? And why does this need instead of seeking to appease itself in acts of violence, by amorous adventures, or in debauch, choose precisely to satisfy itself symbolically? And why does Flaubert turn to writing rather than to painting or music for this symbolic satisfaction; he could just as well not resort to the artistic field at all (there is also mysticism, for example). "I could have been a great actor," wrote Flaubert somewhere. Why did he not try to be one? In a word, we have understood nothing; we have seen a succession of accidental happenings, of desires springing forth fully armed, one from the other, with no possibility for us to grasp their genesis. The *transitions,* the becomings, the transformations, have been carefully veiled from us, and we

have been limited to putting order into the
succession by invoking empirically established but literally unintelligible sequences
(the need to act preceding in the adolescent
the need to write). Yet this is called psychology! Open any biography at random, and this
is the kind of description which you will find
more or less interspersed with accounts of
external events and allusions to the great
idols of our epoch—heredity, education, environment, physiological constitution. Oc-
casionally, in the better works the connection
established between antecedent and conse-
quent or between two concomitant desires
and their reciprocal action is not conceived
merely as a type of regular sequence; sometimes it is "comprehensible" in the sense
which Jaspers understands in his general
treatment of psychopathology. But this comprehension remains a grasp of general connections. For example we will realize the link
between chastity and mysticism, between
fainting and hypocrisy. But we are ignorant
always of the concrete relation between *this*
chastity (this abstinence in relation to a particular woman, *this* struggle against a definite
temptation) and the individual content of
the mysticism; in the same way psychiatry is
too quickly satisfied when it throws light on
the general structures of delusions and does
not seek to comprehend the individual, con-

crete content of the psychoses (why this man believes himself to be that particular histori- cal personality rather than some other; why his compensatory delusion is satisfied with specifically these ideas of grandeur instead of others, *etc.*).

But most important of all, these "psycho- logical" explanations refer us ultimately to inexplicable original data. These are the sim- ple bodies of psychology. We are told, for ex- ample, that Flaubert had a "grandiose ambi- tion" and all of the previously quoted descrip- tion depends on this original ambition. So far so good. But this ambition is an irreducible fact which by no means satisfies the mind. The irreducibility here has no justification other than refusal to push the analysis further. The fact cited is given as basic, and that is where the psychologist stops. This is why we experience a troubled feeling of min- gled resignation and dissatisfaction when we read these psychological treatises. "See," we say to ourselves, "Flaubert was ambitious. He was that kind of man." It would be as futile to ask why he was such as to seek to know why he was tall and blond. Of course we have to stop somewhere; it is the very contingency of all real existence. This rock is covered with moss, the rock next to it is not. Gustave Flaubert had literary ambition, and his brother Achille lacked it. That's the way it is. In the same way we want to know the properties of phosphorus, and we attempt to reduce them to the structure of the chemical molecules which compose it. But why are there molecules of this type? That's the way it is, that's all. The explanation of Flaubert's psychology will consist, if it is possible, in referring the complexity of his behaviour patterns, his feelings, and his tastes back to certain *properties*, comparable to those of chemical bodies, beyond which it would be foolish to attempt to proceed. Yet we feel obscurely that Flaubert had not "received" his ambition. It is meaningful; therefore it is free. Neither heredity, nor bourgeois background nor education can account for it, still less those physiological considerations regarding the "nervous temperament," which have been the vogue for some time now. The nerve is not *meaningful;* it is a colloidal substance which can be described in itself and which does not have the quality of transcendence; that is, it does not identify itself by means of other realities as being what it is. Under no circumstances could the nerve furnish the basis for meaning. In one sense Flaubert's ambition is a fact with all a fact's contingency—and it is true that it is impossible to advance beyond that fact—but in another sense it *makes itself,* and our satisfaction is a guarantee to us that we may be able to grasp beyond this ambition something more, something like a radical decision which, without ceasing to be contingent, would be the veritable psychic irreducible.

What we are demanding then—and what nobody ever attempts to give us—is a *veritable* irreducible; that is, an irreducible of which the irreducibility would be self-evident, which would not be presented as the postulate of the psychologist and the result of his refusal or his incapacity to go further, but which when established would produce in us an accompanying feeling of satisfaction. This demand on our part does not come from that ceaseless pursuit of a cause, that infinite regression which has often been described as constitutive of rational research and which consequently—far from being exclusively associated with psychological investigation, may be found in all disciplines and in all problems. This is not the childish quest of a "because," which allows no further "why?" It is on the contrary a demand based on a preontological comprehension of human reality and on the related refusal to consider man as capable of being analyzed and reduced to original data, to determined desires (or "drives"), supported by the subject as properties by an object. Even if we were to consider him as such, it would be necessary to choose: either *Flaubert,* the man, whom we can love or detest, blame or praise, who represents for us *the other,* who directly attacks our being by the very fact that he has existed, would be originally a substratum unqualified by these desires; that is, a sort of indeterminate clay which would have to receive them passively—or he would be reduced to the simple bundle of these irreducible drives or tendencies. In either case the *man* disappears; we can no longer find *"the one" to whom* this or that experience has *happened;* either in looking for the *person,* we encounter a useless, contradictory metaphysical substance—or else the being whom we seek vanishes in a dust of phenomena bound together by external connections. But what each one of us requires in his very effort to comprehend another is that he should never have to resort to this idea of substance, which is inhuman because it is well this side of the human. Finally the fact is that the being considered does not crumble into dust, and one can discover in him that unity—for which substance was only a caricature—which must be a unity of responsibility, a unity agreeable or hateful, blamable and praiseworthy, in short *personal.* This unity, which is the being of the man under consideration, is a *free unification,* and this unification can not come *after* a diversity which it unifies.

But *to be,* for Flaubert, as for every subject of "biography," means to be unified in the world. The irreducible unification which we ought to find, which is Flaubert, and which we require biographers to reveal to us—this is the unification of an *original project,* a unification which should reveal itself to us as a *non-substantial absolute.* Therefore we should forego these so-called irreducible details and taking the very evidence of them for a criterion, not stop in our investigation before it is evident that we neither can nor ought to go any further. In particular we must avoid trying to reconstruct a person by means of his inclinations, just as Spinoza warns us not to attempt to reconstruct substance or its attributes by the summation of its modes. Every desire if presented as an irreducible is an absurd contingency and involves in absurdity human reality taken as a whole. For example, if I declare of one of my friends that he "likes to go rowing," I deliberately intend to stop my investigation there. But on the other hand, I thus establish a contingent *fact,* which nothing can explain and which, though it has the gratuity of free decision, by no means has its autonomy. I can not in fact consider this fondness for rowing as the fundamental project of Pierre; it contains something secondary and derived. Those who portray a character in this way by successive strokes come close to holding that each of these strokes—each one of the desires confronted—is bound to the others by connections which are purely contingent and simply external. Those who, on the other hand, try to explain this liking will fall into the view of what Comte called *materialism;* that is, of explaining the higher by the lower. Someone will say, for example, that the subject considered is a sportsman, who likes violent exercise and is in addition a man of the outdoors who especially likes open air sports. He will want to explain more general and less differentiated tendencies under the heading of the desire, which stands in exactly the same relation to them as the zoological species does to the genus. Thus the psychological explanation when it does not suddenly decide to stop, is sometimes the mere putting into relief relations of pure concomitance or of constant succession and it is at other times a simple classification. To explain Pierre's fondness for rowing is to make it a member of the family of fondness for open air sports and to attach this family to that of fondness for sport in general. Moreover we will be able to find still more general and barren rubrics if we classify the taste for sports as one aspect of the love of chance, which will itself be given as a specific instance of the fundamental fondness for play. It is obvious that this so-called explanatory classification has no more value or interest than the classifications in ancient botany; like the latter it amounts to assuming the priority of the abstract over the concrete— as if the fondness for play existed first in general to be subsequently made specific by the action of these circumstances in the love of sport, the latter in the fondness for rowing, and finally the rowing in the desire to row on a particular stream, under certain circumstances in a particular season—and like the ancient classifications it fails to explain the concrete enrichment which at each stage is undergone by the abstract inclination considered.

Furthermore how are we to believe that a desire to row is *only* a desire to row. Can we truthfully admit that it can be reduced so simply to what it is? The most discerning moralists have shown how a desire reaches beyond itself. Pascal believed that he could discover in hunting, for example, or tennis, or in a hundred other occupations, the need of being diverted. He revealed that in an activity which would be absurd if reduced to itself, there was a meaning which transcended it; that is, an indication which referred to the reality of man in general and to his condition. Similarly Stendhal in spite of his attachment to ideologists, and Proust in spite of his intellectualistic and analytical tendencies, have shown that love and jealousy can not be reduced to the strict desire of possessing a *particular* woman, but that these emotions aim at laying hold of the world in its entirety through the woman. This is the meaning of Stendhal's crystallization, and it is precisely for this reason that love as Stendhal describes it appears as a mode of being in the world. Love is a fundamental relation of the for-itself to the world and to itself (selfness) through a particular woman; the woman represents only a conducting body which is placed in the circuit. These analyses may be inexact or only partially true; nevertheless they make us suspect a method other than pure analytical description. In the same way Catholic novelists in writing of carnal love have commented on it as a surpassing toward God—in Don Juan, "the eternally unsatisfied," in sin, "the place empty of God." There is no question here of finding again an abstract behind the concrete; the impulse toward God is no *less concrete* than the impulse toward a particular woman. On the contrary, it is a matter of rediscovering under the partial and incomplete aspects of the subject the veritable concreteness which can be only the totality of its impulse toward being, its original relation to itself, to the world, and to the Other, in the unity of internal relations and of a fundamental project. This impulse can be only purely individual and unique. Far from estranging us from the person, as Bourget's analysis, for example, does in constituting the individual by means of a summation of general maxims, this impulse will not lead us to find in the need of writing—and of writing particular books—the need of activity in general. On the contrary, rejecting equally the theory of malleable clay and that of the bundle of drives, we will discover the individual person in the initial project which constitutes him. It is for this reason that the irreducibility of the result attained will be revealed as self-evident, not because it is the poorest and the most abstract but because it is the richest. The intuition here will be accompanied by an individual fullness.

The problem poses itself in approximately these terms: If we admit that the person is a totality, we can not hope to reconstruct him by an addition or by an organization of the diverse tendencies which we have empirically discovered in him. On the contrary, in each inclination, in each tendency the person expresses himself completely, although from a different angle, a little as Spinoza's substance expresses itself completely in each of its attributes. But if this is so, we should discover in each tendency, in each attitude of the subject, a meaning which transcends it. A jealousy of a particular date in which a subject posits himself in history in relation to a certain woman, signifies for the one who knows how to interpret it, the total relation to the world by which the subject constitutes himself as a self. In other words this *empirical* attitude is by itself the expression of the "choice of an intelligible character." There is no mystery about this. We no longer have to do with an intelligible pattern which can be present in our thought only, while we apprehend and conceptualize the unique pattern of the subject's empirical existence. If the empirical attitude signifies the choice of the intelligible character, it is because it is *itself* this choice. Indeed the distinguishing characteristic of the intelligible choice, as we shall see later, is that it can exist only as the transcendent meaning of each concrete, empirical choice. It is by no means first effected in some unconscious or on the noumenal level to be *subsequently* expressed in a particular observable attitude; there is not even an *ontological* preeminence over the empirical choice, but it is on principle that which must always detach itself from the empirical choice as its *beyond* and the infinity of its transcendence. Thus if I am rowing on the river, I am nothing—either here or in any other world— save this concrete project of rowing. But this project itself inasmuch as it is the totality of my being, expresses my original choice in particular circumstances; it is nothing other than the choice of myself as a totality in these circumstances. That is why a special method must aim at detaching the fundamental meaning which the project admits and which can be only the individual secret of the subject's being-in-the-world. It is then rather by a *comparison* of the various empirical drives of a subject that we try to discover and disengage the fundamental project which is common to them all—and not by a simple summation or reconstruction of these tendencies; each drive or tendency is the entire person.

There is naturally an infinity of possible projects as there is an infinity of possible human beings. Nevertheless, if we are to recognize certain common characteristics among them and if we are going to attempt to classify them in larger categories, it is best first to undertake individual investigations in the cases which we can study more easily. In our research, we will be guided by this principle: to stop only in the presence of evident irreducibility; that is, never to believe that we have reached the initial project until the projected end appears as *the very being* of the subject under consideration. This is why we can not stop at those classifications of "authentic project" and "unauthentic project of the self" which Heidegger wishes to establish. In addition to the fact that such a classification, in spite of its author's intent, is tainted with an ethical concern shown by its very terminology, it is based on the attitude of the subject

toward his own death. Now if death causes
anguish, and if consequently we can either
flee the anguish or throw ourselves resolutely
into it, it is a truism to say that this is because
we wish to hold on to life. Consequently anguish before death and resolute decision or
flight into unauthenticity can not be considered as fundamental projects of our being.
On the contrary, they can be understood only
on the foundation of an original project of
living; that is, on an original choice of our
being. It is right then in each case to pass beyond the results of Heidegger's interpretation
toward a still more fundamental project.

This fundamental project must not of
course refer to any other and should be conceived by itself. It can be concerned neither
with death nor life nor any particular characteristic of the human condition; the original
project of a for-itself *can aim only at its
being.*[4] The project of being or desire of
being or drive toward being does not originate in a physiological differentiation or in
an empirical contingency; in fact it is not
distinguished from the being of the for-itself.
The for-itself is a being, the nature of which
is to question its own being in the form of a
project of being. To the for-itself *being* means
to make known what one is by means of a pos-

[4] For an explanation of technical terms used in this
section see introduction. Tr.

sibility appearing as a value. Possibility and value belong to the being of the for-itself. The for-itself is defined ontologically as a *lack of being,* and possibility belongs to the for-itself as *that which it lacks,* in the same way that value haunts the for-itself as the totality of being which is lacking. What we have expressed in Part Two in terms of lack can be just as well expressed in terms of *freedom.* The for-itself chooses because it is lack; freedom is really synonymous with lack. Freedom is the mode of concrete being of the lack of being. Ontologically then it amounts to the same thing to say that value and possibility exist as internal limits of a lack of being which can exist only as a lack of being—or that the upsurge of freedom determines its possibility and thereby limits *its* value. Thus we can advance no further but have encountered the self-evident irreducible when we have reached the *project of being,* for obviously it is impossible to advance further than *being* and there is no difference between the project of being, possibility, value, on the one hand, and *being,* on the other. Fundamentally man is *the desire to be,* and the existence of this desire is not to be established by an empirical induction; it is the result of an *a priori* description of the being of the for-itself, since desire is a lack and since the for-itself is the being which is to itself its own lack of being. The original project which is expressed in each of our empirically observable tendencies is then the *project of being;* or, if you prefer, each empirical tendency exists with the original project of being, in a relation of expression and symbolic satisfaction just as conscious drives, with Freud, exist in relation to the complex and to the original libido. Moreover the desire to be by no means exists *first* in order to cause itself to be expressed subsequently by desires *a posteriori.* There is nothing outside of the symbolic expression which it finds in concrete desires. There is not first a single desire of being, then a thousand particular feelings, but the desire to be exists and manifests itself only in and through jealousy, greed, love of art, cowardice, courage, and a thousand contingent, empirical expressions which always cause human reality to appear to us only as *manifested* by a *particular man,* by a specific person.

As for the being which is the object of this desire, we know *a priori* what this is. The for-itself is the being which is to itself its own lack of being. The being which the for-itself lacks is the in-itself. The for-itself arises as the annihilation of the in-itself and this annihilation is defined as the project toward the in-itself. Between the annihilated in-itself and the projected in-itself the for-itself is nothingness. Thus the end and the goal of the annihilation which I am is the in-itself. Thus human reality is the desire of being in-itself. But the in-itself which it desires can not be pure contingent, absurd in-itself, comparable at every point to that which it encounters and which it annihilates. The annihilation, as we have seen, is in fact similar to a revolt of the in-itself, which annihilates itself against its contingency. To say that the for-itself lives its facticity, as we have seen in the chapter concerning the body, amounts to saying that the annihilation is the vain effort of a being to establish its own being and that it is the withdrawal to establish which provokes the minute displacement by which nothingness enters into being. The being which forms the object of the desire of the for-itself is then an in-itself which would be to itself its own foundation; that is, which would be to its facticity in the same relation as the for-itself is to its motivations. In addition the for-itself, being the negation of the in-itself could not desire the pure and simple return to the in-itself. Here as with Hegel, the negation of the negation can not bring us back to our point of departure. Quite the contrary, what the for-itself demands of the in-itself is precisely the totality detotalized—"In-itself annihilated in for-itself." In other words the for-itself projects *being as for-itself,* a being which is what it is. It is as being which is what it is not, and which is not what it is, that the for-itself projects being what it is. It is as consciousness that it wishes to have the impermeability and infinite density of the in-itself. It is as annihilation of the in-itself and a perpetual evasion of contingency and of facticity that it wishes to be its own foundation. This is why possibility is projected in general as what is lacking to the for-itself in order to become in-itself-for-itself. The fundamental value which presides over this project is exactly the in-itself-for-itself; that is, the ideal of a consciousness which would be the foundation of its own being-in-itself by the pure consciousness which it would take of itself. It is this ideal which can be called God. Thus the best way to conceive of the fundamental project of human reality is to say that man is the being whose project is to become God. Whatever may be the myths and rites of the religion considered, God is first "sensible to the heart" of man as the one who identifies and defines him in his ultimate and fundamental project. If man possesses a preontological comprehension of the being of God, it is not the great wonders of nature nor the power of society which have conferred it upon him. God, value and supreme end of transcendence, represents the permanent limit in terms of which man makes known what he is. To be man means to reach toward being God. Or if you prefer, man fundamentally is the desire to be God.

It may be asked, if man on coming into the world is borne toward God as toward his limit, if he can choose only to be God, what becomes of freedom? For freedom is nothing other than a choice which creates for itself its own possibilities, but it appears here that the initial project of being God, which "defines" man, comes close to being the same as a human "nature" or an "essence." The answer is that while the *meaning* of the desire is ultimately the project of being God, the desire is never *constituted* by this meaning; on the contrary, it always represents a particular discovery of its ends. These ends in fact are pursued in terms of a particular empirical situation, and it is this very pursuit which constitutes the surroundings *as a situation*. The desire of being is always realized as the desire of a mode of being. And this desire of a mode of being expresses itself in turn as the meaning of the myriads of concrete desires which constitute the web of our conscious life. Thus we find ourselves before very complex symbolic structures which have *at least* three stories. In empirical desire I can discern a symbolization of a fundamental concrete desire which is the person himself and which represents the mode in which he has decided to put his own being into question. This fundamental desire in turn expresses concretely

in the world within the particular situation
enveloping the individual, an abstract meaningful structure which is the desire of being
in general; it ought to be considered as human reality in the person, and it brings about
his community with others, thus making it
possible to state that there is a truth concerning man and not only concerning individuals
who cannot be compared. Absolute concreteness, completion, existence as a totality belong then to the free and fundamental desire
which is the unique person. Empirical desire
is only a symbolization of this; it refers to this
and derives its meaning from it while remaining partial and reducible, for the empirical
desire can not be conceived in isolation. On
the other hand, the desire of being in its abstract purity is the *truth* of the concrete fundamental desire, but it does not exist by virtue of reality. Thus the fundamental project,
the person, the free realization of human
truth is everywhere in all desires (save for
those exceptions treated in the preceding
chapter, concerning, for example, "indiffer-
ents"). It is never apprehended except
through desires—as we can apprehend space
only through bodies which shape it for us,
though space is a specific reality and not a
concept. Or, if you like, it is like the *object*
of Husserl, which reveals itself only by
"Abschattungen," and which nevertheless

does not allow itself to be absorbed by any one *Abschattung*. We can understand after these remarks that the abstract, onto-logical "desire to be" is unable to represent the fundamental, *human* structure of the individual; it cannot be an obstacle to his free-dom. Freedom in fact, as we have shown in the preceding chapter, is strictly identified with annihilation. The only being which can be called free is the being which annihilates its being. Moreover we know that annihila-tion is *lack of being* and can not be other-wise. Freedom is precisely the being which makes itself a lack of being. But since desire, as we have established, is identical with lack of being, freedom can arise only as being which makes itself a desire of being; that is, as the project-for-itself of being in-itself-for-itself. Here we have arrived at an abstract structure which can by no means be consid-ered as the nature or essence of freedom. Freedom is existence, and in it existence pre-cedes essence. The upsurge of freedom is im-mediate and concrete and is not to be dis-tinguished from its choice; that is, from the person himself. But the structure under con-sideration can be called the *truth* of freedom; that is, it is the human meaning of freedom.

It should be possible to establish the human truth of the person, as we have at-tempted to do, by an ontological phenomenology. The catalogue of empirical desires ought to be made the object of appropriate psychological investigations; observation and induction and, as needed, experience can serve to draw up this list. They will indicate to the philosopher the comprehensible relations which can unite to each other various desires and various patterns of behaviours, and will bring to light certain concrete connections between the subject of experience and "situations" experientially defined (which at bottom originate only from limitations applied in the name of positivity to the fundamental situation of the subject in the world). But in establishing and classifying fundamental desires or *individual persons* neither of these methods is appropriate. Actually there can be no question of determining *a priori* and ontologically what appears in all the unpredictability of a free act. This is why we shall limit ourselves here to indicating very summarily the possibilities of such a quest and its perspectives. The very fact that we can subject any man whatsoever to such an investigation—that is what belongs to human reality in general. Or, if you prefer, this is what can be established by an ontology. But the inquiry itself and its results are on principle wholly outside the possibilities of an ontology.

On the other hand, pure, simple empirical

description can only give us catalogues and put us in the presence of pseudo-irreducibles (the desire to write, to swim, a taste for adventure, jealousy, *etc.*). It is not enough in fact to draw up a list of behaviour patterns, of tendencies and inclinations, it is necessary also to *decipher* them; that is, it is necessary to know how to *question* them. This research can be conducted only according to the rules of a specific method. It is this method which we call existential psychoanalysis.

The *goal* of psychoanalysis is to *decipher* the empirical behaviour patterns of man; that is to bring out in the open the revelations which each one of them contains and to fix them conceptually.

Its *point of departure* is *experience;* its pillar of support is the fundamental, preontological comprehension which man has of the human person. Although the majority of people can well ignore the indications contained in a gesture, a word, a sign and can look with scorn on the revelation which they carry, each human individual nevertheless possesses *a priori* the *meaning* of the revelatory value of these manifestations and is capable of deciphering them, at least if he is aided and guided by a helping hand. Here as elsewhere, truth is not encountered by chance; it does not belong to a domain where one must seek it without ever having any presentiment of its location, as one can go to look for the source of the Nile or of the Niger. It belongs *a priori* to human comprehension and the essential task is an hermeneutic; that is, a deciphering, a determination, and a conceptualization.

Its method is comparative. Since each example of human conduct symbolizes in its own manner the fundamental choice which must be brought to light, and since at the same time each one disguises this choice under its occasional character and its historical opportunity, only the comparison of these acts of conduct can effect the emergence of the unique revelation which they all express in a different way. The first outline of this method has been furnished for us by the psychoanalysis of Freud and his disciples. For this reason it will be profitable here to indicate more specifically the points where existential psychoanalysis will be inspired by psychoanalysis proper and those where it will radically differ from it.

Both kinds of psychoanalysis consider all objectively discernible manifestations of "psychic life" as maintaining the relation of symbolization and symbol to the fundamental, total structures which constitute the individual person. Both consider that there are no original data such as hereditary dispositions, character, *etc.* Existential psychoanal-

ysis recognizes nothing *before* the original upsurge of human freedom; empirical psychoanalysis holds that the original affectivity of
the individual is virgin wax *before* its history.
The libido is nothing besides its concrete fixa-
tions, save for a permanent possibility of fixing anything whatsoever upon anything whatsoever. Both consider the human being as a
perpetual, searching, living process of history.
Rather than uncovering static, constant data,
they discover the meaning, orientation, and
adventures of this history. Due to this fact,
both consider man in the world and do not
imagine that one can question the being of a
man without accounting for all his *situation*.
Psychological investigations aim at recon-
stituting the life of the subject from birth to
the moment of the cure; they utilize all the
objective documentation which they can
find; letters, witnesses, intimate diaries,
"social" information of every kind. What they
aim at restoring is less a pure psychic event
than a framework; the crucial event of in-
fancy and the psychic crystallization around
this event. Here again we have to do with a
situation. Each "historical" fact from this
point of view will be considered at once as a
factor of the psychic evolution and as a *symbol* of that evolution. For it is nothing in itself.
It operates only according to the way in which

it is taken and this very manner of taking it expresses symbolically the internal disposition of the individual.

Empirical psychoanalysis and existential psychoanalysis both search within an existing situation for a fundamental attitude which can not be expressed by simple, logical definitions because it is prior to all logic, and which requires reconstruction according to the laws of specific syntheses. Empirical psychoanalysis seeks to determine the *complex,* the very name of which indicates the polyvalence of all the meanings which are referred back to it. Existential psychoanalysis seeks to determine the *original choice.* This original choice operating in the face of the world and being a choice of position in the world is total like the complex; it is prior to logic like the complex. It is this which decides the attitude of the person when confronted with logic and principles; therefore there can be no possibility of questioning it in conformance to logic. It brings together in a prelogical synthesis the totality of the existent, and as such it is the center of reference for an infinity of polyvalent meanings.

Both our psychoanalyses refuse to admit that the subject is in a privileged position to proceed in these inquiries concerning himself. They equally insist on a strictly objective method, using as documentary evidence the data of reflection as well as the testimony of others. Of course the subject *can* undertake a psychoanalytic investigation of himself. But in this case he must renounce at the outset all benefit stemming from his peculiar position and must question himself exactly as if he were someone else. Empirical psychoanalysis in fact is based on the hypothesis of the existence of an unconscious psyche, which on principle escapes the intuition of the subject. Existential psychoanalysis rejects the hypothesis of the unconscious; it makes the psychic act coextensive with consciousness. But if the fundamental project is fully experienced by the subject and hence wholly conscious, that certainly does not mean that it must by the same token be *known* by him; quite the contrary. The reader will perhaps recall the care we took in the Introduction to distinguish between consciousness and knowledge. To be sure, as we have seen earlier, reflection can be considered as a quasi-knowledge. But what it grasps at each moment is not the pure project of the for-itself as it is symbolically expressed—often in several ways at once—by the concrete behaviour which it apprehends. It grasps the concrete behaviour itself; that is, the specific dated desire in all its characteristic network. It grasps at once symbol and symbolization. This apprehension, to be sure, is entirely constituted by a preontological comprehension of the fundamental project; better yet, in so far as the reflection is almost a non-thetic consciousness of itself as reflection, it *is* this same project, as well as the non-reflective consciousness. But it does not follow that it commands the instruments and techniques necessary to isolate the choice symbolized, to fix it by concepts, and to bring it forth into the full light of day. It is penetrated by a great light without being able to express what this light is illuminating. We are not dealing with an unsolved riddle as the Freudians believe; all is there, luminous, reflection is in full possession of it, apprehends all. But this "mystery in broad daylight" is due to the fact that this possession is deprived of the means which would ordinarily permit *analysis* and *conceptualization*. It grasps everything, all at once, without shading, without relief, without connections of grandeur— not that these shades, these values, these reliefs exist somewhere and are hidden from it, but rather because they must be established by another human attitude and because they can exist only *by means of* and *for* knowledge. Reflection, unable to serve as the basis for existential psychoanalysis, will then simply furnish us with the brute materials toward which the psychoanalyst must take an objective attitude. Thus only will he be able to *know* what he *already understands*.

The result is that complexes uprooted from the depths of the unconscious, like projects revealed by existential psychoanalysis, will be apprehended *from the point of view of another*. Consequently the *object* thus brought into the light will be articulated according to the structures of the transcended-transcendence; that is, its being will be the being-for-another even if the psychoanalyst and the subject of the psychoanalysis are actually the same person. Thus the project which is brought to light by either kind of psychoanalysis can be only the totality of the individual human being, the irreducible element of the transcendence with the structure of *being-for-others*. What always escapes these methods of investigation is the project as it is for itself, the complex in its own being. This project-for-itself can be experienced only as a living possession; there is an incompatibility between existence for-itself and objective existence. But the object of the two psychoanalyses has in it nonetheless the *reality of a being;* the subject's knowledge of it can in addition contribute to *clarify* reflection, and that reflection can then become possession which will be a quasi-knowing.

At this point the similarity between the two kinds of psychoanalysis ceases. They differ fundamentally in that empirical psychoanalysis has decided upon its own irreducible instead of allowing this to make itself known in a self-evident intuition. The libido or the will to power in actuality constitutes a psychobiological residue which is not clear in itself and which does not appear to us as *being beforehand* the irreducible limit of the investigation. Finally it is experience which establishes that the foundation of complexes is this libido or this will to power, and these results of empirical inquiry are perfectly contingent, they are not convincing. Nothing prevents our conceiving *a priori* of a "human reality" which would not be expressed by the will to power, for which the libido would not constitute the original, undifferentiated project. On the other hand, the choice to which existential psychoanalysis will lead us, precisely because it is a choice, accounts for its original contingency, for the contingency of the choice is the obverse of its freedom. Furthermore, inasmuch as it is established on the *lack of being,* conceived as a fundamental characteristic of being, it receives its legitimacy *as a choice,* and we know that we do not have to push further. Each result then will be at once fully contingent and legitimately irreducible. Moreover it will always remain *particular;* that is, we will not achieve as the ultimate goal of our investigation and the foundation of all behaviour patterns, an abstract, general term, libido for example, which would be differentiated and made concrete first in complexes and then in detailed acts of conduct, due to the action of external facts and the history of the subject. On the contrary, it will be a choice which remains unique and which is from the start absolute concreteness. Details of behaviour can express or *particularize* this choice, but they can not make it more concrete than it already is. That is because the choice is nothing other than the *being* of each human reality; this amounts to saying that a particular partial behaviour *is* or expresses the original choice of this human reality since for human reality there is no difference between existing and choosing for itself. From this fact we understand that existential psychoanalysis does not have to proceed from the fundamental "complex," which is exactly the choice of being, to an abstraction like the libido which would explain it. The complex is the ultimate choice, it is the choice of being and *makes itself such.* Bringing it into the light will reveal it each time as evidently irreducible. It follows necessarily that the libido and the will to power will appear to existential psychoanalysis neither as general characteristics common to all mankind nor as irreducibles. At most it will be possible after the investigation to establish that they express by virtue of particular ensembles in certain subjects a fundamental choice which can not be reduced to either one of them. We have seen in fact that desire and sexuality in general express an original effort of the for-itself to recover its being which has become estranged through contact with another. The will to power also originally supposes being for another, the comprehension of another, and the choice of winning its own salvation by means of the other. The foundation of this attitude must be an original choice which would make us understand the radical identification of being-in-it-self-for-itself with being-for-others.

The fact that the ultimate term of this existential inquiry must be a *choice*, distinguishes even better the psychoanalysis for which we have outlined the method and principal features. It thereby renounces the supposition that the environment acts mechanically on the subject under consideration. The environment can act on the subject only to the exact extent that he comprehends it; that is, transforms it into a situation. Hence no objective description of this environment could be of any use to us. From the start the environment conceived as a situation refers to the for-itself which is choosing, just as the for-itself refers to the environment by the very fact that it is in the world. By renouncing all mechanical causation, we renounce at the same time all *general* interpretation of the symbolization confronted. Our goal could not be to establish empirical laws of succession, nor could we constitute a universal symbolism. Rather the psychoanalyst will have to rediscover at each step a symbol functioning in the particular case which he is considering. If each being is a totality, it is not conceivable that there can exist elementary symbolic relationships (*e.g.* the faeces = gold, or a pin-cushion = the breast) which preserve a constant meaning in all cases; that is, which remain unaltered when they pass from one meaningful ensemble to another ensemble. Furthermore the psychoanalyst will never lose sight of the fact that the choice is living and consequently can be *recalled* by the subject who is being studied. We have shown in the preceding chapter the importance of the instant which represents abrupt changes in orientation and the assuming of a new posi-tion in the face of an unalterable past. From this moment on, we must always be ready to consider that symbols change meaning and to abandon the symbol used hitherto. Thus existential psychoanalysis will have to be completely flexible and adapt itself to the slightest observable changes in the subject. Our concern here is to understand what is *individual* and often even instantaneous. The method which has served for one subject will not necessarily be suitable to use for another subject or for the same subject at a later period.

Precisely because the goal of the inquiry must be to discover a *choice* and not a *state,* the investigator must recall on every occasion that his object is not a datum buried in the darkness of the unconscious but a free, conscious determination—which is not even resident in consciousness, but which is one with this consciousness itself. Empirical psychoanalysis, to the extent that its method is better than its principles, is often in sight of an existential discovery, but it always stops part way. When it thus approaches the fundamental choice, the resistance of the subject collapses suddenly and he *recognizes* the image of himself which is presented to him as if he were seeing himself in a mirror. This involuntary testimony of the subject is precious for the psychoanalyst; he sees there the sign that he has reached his goal; he can pass on from the investigation proper to the cure. But nothing in his principles or in his initial postulates permits him to understand or to utilize this testimony. Where could he get any such right? If the complex is really unconscious—that is, if there is a barrier separating the sign from the thing signified—how could the subject *recognize* it? Does the unconscious complex recognize itself? But haven't we been told that it lacks *understanding?* And if of ne·

cessity we granted to it the faculty of understanding the signs, would this not be to make
of it by the same token a conscious unconscious? What is understanding if not to be
conscious of what is understood? Shall we say
on the other hand that it is the subject as conscious who recognizes the image presented?
But how could he compare it with his true
state since that is out of reach and since he has
never had any knowledge of it? At most he
will be able to judge that the psychoanalytic
explanation of his case is a *probable* hypothesis, which derives its probability from
the number of behaviour patterns which it
explains. His relation to this interpretation is
that of a third party, that of the psychoanalyst himself; he has no privileged position. And if he *believes* in the probability of
the psychoanalytic hypothesis, is this simple
belief, which lives in the limits of his consciousness, able to effect the breakdown of
the barriers which dam up the unconscious
tendencies? The psychoanalyst doubtless has
some obscure picture of an abrupt coincidence of conscious and unconscious. But he
has removed all methods of conceiving of this
coincidence in any positive sense.

Still, the enlightenment of the subject is a
fact. There is an intuition here which is accompanied with evidence. The subject guided
by the psychoanalyst does more and better

than to give his agreement to an hypothesis; he touches it, he sees what it is. This is truly understandable only if the subject has never ceased being conscious of his deep tendencies; better yet, only if these drives are not distinguished from his conscious self. In this case as we have seen, the traditional psychoanalytic interpretation does not cause him to assume *consciousness* of what he is; it causes him to assume *knowledge* of what he is. It is existential psychoanalysis then which claims the final intuition of the subject as decisive.

This comparison allows us to understand better what an existential psychoanalysis must be if it is entitled to exist. It is a method destined to bring to light, in a strictly objective form, the subjective choice by which each living person makes himself a person; that is, makes known to himself what he is. Since what the method seeks is a *choice of being* at the same time as a *being,* it must reduce particular behaviour patterns to fundamental relations—not of sexuality or of will to power, but of *being*—which are expressed in this behaviour. It is then guided from the start toward a comprehension of being and must not assign itself any other goal than to discover being and the mode of being of the being confronting this being. It is forbidden to stop before attaining this goal. It will utilize the comprehension of being which characterizes the investigator inasmuch as he is himself a human reality; and as it seeks to detach being from its symbolic expressions, it will have to rediscover each time on the basis of a comparative study of acts and attitudes, a symbol destined to decipher them. Its criterion of success will be the number of facts which its hypothesis permits it to explain and to unify as well as the self-evident intuition of the irreducibility of the end attained. To this criterion will be added in all cases where it is possible, the decisive testimony of the subject. The results thus achieved—that is, the ultimate ends of the individual—can then become the object of a classification, and it is by the comparison of these results that we will be able to establish general considerations about human reality as an empirical choice of its own ends. The behaviour studied by this psychoanalysis will include not only dreams, failures, obsessions, and neuroses, but also and especially the thoughts of waking life, successfully adjusted acts, style, *etc.* This psychoanalysis has not yet found its Freud. At most we can find the foreshadowing of it in certain particularly successful biographies. We hope to be able to attempt elsewhere two examples in relation to Flaubert and Dostoevsky. But it matters little to us whether it now exists; the important thing is that it is possible.

II

THE MEANING OF "TO MAKE" AND "TO HAVE": POSSESSION

THE INFORMATION which ontology can furnish concerning behaviour patterns and desire must serve as the basic principles of existential psychoanalysis. This does not mean that there is an over-all pattern of abstract desires common to all men; it means that concrete desires have structures which emerge during the study of ontology because each desire—the desire of eating or of sleeping as well as the desire of creating a work of art—expresses all human reality. As I have shown elsewhere,[1] the knowledge of man must be a totality; empirical, partial pieces of knowledge on this level lack all significance. We shall succeed in our task if we utilize the fragments of knowledge achieved up to this point,

[1] *Esquisse d'une théorie phénoménologique des émotions.* Herman Caul, 1939. In English *The Psychology of Imagination.* Philosophical Library, 1948.

for laying down the bases for existential psychoanalysis. Indeed this is the point where
ontology must stop; its final discoveries are
the first principles of psychoanalysis. Henceforth we must have another method since the
object is different. What then does ontology
teach us about desire, since desire is the being
of human reality?

Desire is a lack of being. As such it is directly *supported by* the being of which it is a
lack. This being, as we have said, is the in-
itself-for-itself, consciousness become substance, substance become the cause of itself,
the Man-God. Thus the being of human reality is originally not a substance but an experienced relation. The limiting terms of this relation are first the original In-itself, fixed in
its contingency and its facticity, its essential
characteristic being that it *is,* that it *exists;*
and second the In-itself-for-itself or value,
which exists as the Ideal of the contingent In-
itself and which is characterized as beyond all
contingency and all existence. Man is neither
the one nor the other of these beings, for
strictly speaking, we should never say of him
that he *is* at all. He is what he is not and he is
not what he is; he is the annihilation of the
contingent In-itself which is the cause of itself.
Human reality is the pure effort to become
God without there being any given substratum for that effort, without there being

anything which so endeavours. Desire expresses this endeavour.

Nevertheless desire is not defined solely in relation to the In-itself-cause-of-itself. It is also relative to a brute, concrete existent which we commonly call the object of the desire. This object may be now a slice of bread, now an automobile, now a woman, now an object not yet realized and yet defined—as when the artist desires to create a work of art. Thus by its very structure desire expresses a man's relation to one or several objects in the world; it is one of the aspects of Being-in-the-world. From this point of view we see first that this relation is not of a unique type. It is only by a sort of abbreviation that we speak of "the desire of something." Actually a thousand empirical examples show that we desire to *possess* this object or to *make* that thing or to *be* someone. If I desire this picture, it means that I desire to buy it, to appropriate it for myself. If I desire to write a book, to go for a walk, it means that I desire to "make" this book, to "make" this walk. If I dress up, it is because I desire to *be* well-groomed. I train myself in order to *be* a scientist, *etc.* Thus from the outset, the three big categories of concrete human existence appear to us in their original relation: *to make, to have, to be.*

It is easy to see, however, that the desire to

make is not irreducible. One makes an object
in order to enter into a certain relation with
it. This new relation can be immediately reducible to *having*. For example, I cut a cane
from a branch of a tree (I *make* a cane out of a
branch) in order to *have* this cane. The "making" is reduced to a mode of having. This is
the most common example. But it can also
happen that my activity does not appear on
the surface as reducible. It can appear
gratuitous as in the case of scientific research,
or sport, or aesthetic creation. Yet in these
various examples making is still not irreducible. If I create a picture, a drama, a melody, it
is in order that I may be at the origin of a concrete existence. This existence interests me
only to the degree that the bond of creation
which I establish between it and me gives to
me a particular right of ownership over it. It
is not enough that a certain picture which I
have in mind should exist; it is necessary as
well that it exist *through me*. Evidently in
one sense the ideal would be that I should sustain the picture in being by a sort of continuous creation and that consequently it should
be *mine* as though by a perpetually renewed
emanation. But in another sense it must be
radically distinct from myself—in order that
it may be *mine* but not *me*. Here as in the
Cartesian theory of substances, there is danger
that the being of the created object may be

reabsorbed in my being because of lack of independence and objectivity; hence it must of necessity exist also *in itself,* must perpetually renew its existence *by itself.* Consequently my work appears to me as a continuous creation but fixed in the in-itself; it carries indefinitely my "mark"; that is, it is for an indefinite period "my" thought. Every work of art is a thought, an "idea"; its characteristics are plainly ideal to the extent that it is nothing but a meaning. But on the other hand, this meaning, this thought, which is in one sense perpetually active as if I were perpetually forming it, as if a mind were conceiving it without respite—a mind which would be *my* mind—this thought sustains itself alone in being; it by no means ceases to be active when I am not actually thinking it. I stand to it then in the double relation of the consciousness which conceives it and the consciousness which encounters it. It is precisely this double relation which I express by saying that it is *mine.* We shall see the meaning of it when we have defined precisely the significance of the category "to have." It is in order to enter into this double relation in the synthesis of appropriation that I *create* my work. In fact it is this synthesis of self and not-self (the intimacy and translucency of thought on the one hand and the opaqueness and indifference of the in-itself on the other) that I am aiming

at and which will establish my ownership of
the work. In this sense it is not only strictly
artistic works which I appropriate in this
manner. This cane which I have cut from the
branch is also destined to belong to me in this
double relation: first as an object for everyday use, which is at my disposition and which
I possess as I possess my clothes or my books,
and second as my own work. Thus people who
like to surround themselves with everyday
objects which they themselves have made, are
enjoying subtleties of appropriation. They
unite in a single object and in one syncretism
the appropriation by enjoyment and the appropriation by creation. We find this same
uniting into a single project everywhere from
artistic creation to the cigarette which "is
better when I roll it myself." Later we shall
meet this project in connection with a special
type of ownership which stands as the degradation of it—luxury—for we shall see that
luxury is distinguished not as a quality of the
object possessed but as a quality of possession.

Knowing also—as we showed in the introduction to this fourth part—is a form of appropriation. That is why scientific research is
nothing other than an effort to appropriate.
The truth discovered, like the work of art, is
my knowledge; it is the *noema*[2] of a thought

[2] A term borrowed from Husserl's phenomenology, here
meaning simply "content."

which is discovered only when I form the thought and which consequently appears in a certain mode as maintained in existence by me. It is through me that a facet of the world is revealed; it is to me that it reveals itself. In this sense I am creator and possessor, not that I consider the aspect of being which I discover, as a pure representation, but on the contrary, because this aspect although it is revealed only by me, *exists* profoundly and really. I can say only that I *manifest* it in the sense that Gide tells us that "we always ought to manifest." But I find again an independence analogous to that of the work of art in the character of the *truth* of my thought; that is, in its objectivity. This thought which I form and which derives its existence from me pursues at the same time its own independent existence to the extent that it is *thought by everybody.* It is doubly "I": it is the world revealing itself to me and it is "I" in relation to others, I forming my thought with the mind of others. At the same time it is doubly closed against me: it is the being which I am not (inasmuch as it reveals itself to me) and since it is thought by all from the moment of its appearance, it is a thought devoted to anonymity. This synthesis of self and not-self can be expressed here by the term "mine."

In addition the idea of discovery, of revelation, includes an idea of appropriative enjoyment. What is seen is possessed; to see is to *deflower*. If we examine the comparisons ordinarily used to express the relation between the knower and the known, we see that many of them are represented as being a kind of *violation by sight*. The unknown object given as immaculate, as virgin, comparable to a *whiteness*. It has not yet "delivered up" its secret; man has not yet "snatched" its secret away from it. All these images insist that the object is ignorant of the investigations and the instruments aimed at it; it is unconscious of being known; it goes about its business without noticing the glance which spies on it, like a woman whom a passerby catches unaware at her bath. Figures of speech, sometimes vague, and sometimes more precise, like that of the "unviolated depths" of nature suggest the idea of sexual intercourse more plainly. We speak of snatching away her veils from nature, of unveiling her (*cf.* Schiller's *Veiled Image of Saïs*). Every investigation implies the idea of a nudity which one brings out into the open by clearing away the obstacles which cover it, just as Actaeon clears away the branches so that he can have a better view of Diana at her bath. More than this, knowledge is a hunt. Bacon called it the hunt of Pan. The scientist is the hunter who surprises a white nudity and who violates by looking at it. Thus the totality of these images reveals something which we shall call the *Actaeon complex*.

By taking this idea of the hunt as a guiding thread, we shall discover another symbol of appropriation, perhaps still more primitive: a person hunts for the sake of eating. Curiosity in an animal is always either sexual or alimentary. To know is to devour with the eyes.[3] In fact we can note here, so far as knowledge through the senses is concerned, a process the reverse of that which was discovered in connection with the work of art. We remarked that the work of art is like a fixed emanation of the mind. The mind is continually creating it, and yet it stands alone and indifferent in relation to that creation. This same relation exists in the act of knowing, but its opposite is not excluded. In knowing, consciousness attracts the object to itself and incorporates it in itself. Knowledge is assimilation. The writings of French epistomology swarm with alimentary metaphors (absorption, digestion, assimilation). There is a movement of dissolution which passes from the object to the knowing subject. The known is transformed into *me;* it becomes my thought and thereby consents to receive its existence from me alone. But this movement

[3] For the child, knowing involves actually eating. He wants to taste what he sees. (We might, I suppose, compare Ben Jonson's "Drink to Me Only with Thine Eyes"! Tr.)

of dissolution is fixed by the fact that the known remains in the same place, indefinitely absorbed, devoured, and yet indefinitely intact, wholly digested and yet wholly outside, as indigestible as a stone. For naive imaginations the symbol of the "digested indigestible" is very important; for example, the stone in the stomach of the ostrich or Jonas in the stomach of the whale. The symbol represents the dream of a non-destructive assimilation. It is an unhappy fact—as Hegel noted—that desire destroys its object. In this sense, he said, desire is the desire of devouring. In reaction against this dialectical necessity, the For-itself dreams of an object which may be entirely assimilated by me, which would be *me,* without dissolving into me but still keeping the structure of the *in-itself;* for what I desire exactly is *this* object, and if I eat it, I do not have it any more, I find nothing remaining except myself.

This impossible synthesis of assimilation and an assimilated which maintains its integrity, has deep-rooted connections with basic sexual drives. The idea of "carnal possession" offers us the irritating but seductive figure of a body perpetually possessed and perpetually new, on which possession leaves no trace. This is deeply symbolized in the quality of "smooth" or "polished." What is smooth can be taken and felt but remains no less impenetrable, does not give way in the least beneath the appropriative caress—it is like water. This is the reason why erotic descriptions insist on the smooth whiteness of a woman's body. Smooth—it is what reforms itself under the caress, as water reforms itself in its passage over the stone which has pierced it. At the same time, as we have ·seen earlier, the lover's dream is to identify the beloved object with himself and still preserve for it its own individuality; let the other become me without ceasing to be the other. It is at this point that we encounter the similarity to scientific research: the known object, like the stone in the stomach of the ostrich, is entirely within me, assimilated, transformed into myself, and it is entirely *me;* but at the same time it is impenetrable, untransformable, entirely smooth, with the indifferent nudity of a body which is beloved and caressed in vain. It remains outside; to know it is to devour it yet without consuming it. We see here how the sexual and alimentary currents mingle and interpenetrate in order to constitute the Actaeon complex and the Jonas complex; we can see the digestive and sensual roots which are reunited to give birth to the desire of knowing. Knowledge is at one and the same time a *penetration* and a *superficial* caress, a digestion and the contemplation from afar of an object which will never lose its form, the

production of a thought by a continuous creation and the establishment of the total objective independence of that thought. The
known object is *my thought as a thing*. This
is precisely what I profoundly desire when I
undertake my research—to apprehend my
thought as a thing and the thing as my
thought. The syncretic relation which pro-
vides the basis for the ensemble of such diverse tendencies can be only a relation of *appropriation*. That is why the desire to know,
no matter how disinterested it may appear,
is a relation of appropriation. *To know* is one
of the forms which can be assumed by *to have*.

There remains one type of activity which
we willingly admit is entirely gratuitous; the
activity of *play* and the "drives" which relate
back to it. Can we discover an appropriative
drive in sport? To be sure, it must be noted
first that play as contrasted with the serious
spirit appears to be the least possessive attitude; it strips the real of its reality. The serious attitude involves starting from the world
and attributing more reality to the world
than to oneself; at the very least the serious
man confers reality on himself to the degree
to which he belongs to the world. It is not
by chance that materialism is serious; it is not
by chance that it is found at all times and
places as the favorite doctrine of the revolutionary. This is because revolutionaries are

serious. They come to know themselves first
in terms of the world which oppresses them,
and they wish to change this world. In this
one respect they are in agreement with their
ancient adversaries, the possessors, who also
come to know themselves and appreciate
themselves in terms of their position in the
world. Thus all serious thought is thickened
by the world; it coagulates; it is a dismissal
of human reality in favor of the world. The
serious man is "of the world" and has no re-
source in himself. He does not even imagine
any longer the possibility of *going out of* the
world, for he has given to himself the type of
existence of the rock, the consistency, the
inertia, the opaqueness of the being-in-the-
midst-of-the-world. It is obvious that the serious man at bottom is hiding from himself the
consciousness of his freedom; he is in *bad
faith* and his bad faith aims at presenting
himself to his own eyes as a consequence; everything is a consequence for him, and there
is never any beginning. That is why he is so
concerned with the consequences of his acts.
Marx proposed the original dogma of the serious when he asserted the priority of object
over subject. Man is serious when he takes
himself for an object.

Play, like Kierkegaard's irony, releases subjectivity. What is play indeed if not an activity of which man is the first origin, for which

man himself sets the rules, and which has no consequences except according to the rules posited? As soon as a man apprehends himself as free and wishes to use his freedom, a freedom, by the way, which could just as well be his anguish,[4] then his activity is play. The first principle of play is man himself; through it he escapes his natural nature; he himself sets the value and rules for his acts and consents to play only according to the rules which he himself has established and defined. As a result, there is in a sense "little reality" in the world. It might appear then that when a man is playing, bent on discovering himself as free in his very action, he certainly could not be conncerned with *possessing* a being in the world. His goal, which he aims at through sports or pantomime or games, is to fulfill himself as a certain being, precisely the being who questions his own being. The point of these remarks, however, is not to show us that in play the desire to *make* is irreducible. On the contrary we must conclude that the desire to make is here reduced to a certain desire to be. The act is not its own goal for itself; neither does its explicit end represent its goal and its profound meaning; but the function of the act is to make manifest and to present to *itself* the absolute freedom which is the very being of the person. This particular

[4] See Introduction. Tr.

type of project, which has freedom for its foundation and its goal, deserves a special study. It is radically different from all others in that it aims at a radically different type of being. It would be necessary to explain in full detail its relations with the project of being-God, which has appeared to us as the deep-seated structure of human reality. But such a study can not be made here; it belongs rather to an *Ethics* and it supposes that there has been a preliminary definition of nature and the role of purifying reflection. (Our descriptions have hitherto aimed only at reflection as an *accomplice*); it supposes in addition taking a position which can be *moral* only in the face of values which dwell in the For-itself. Nevertheless the fact remains that the desire to play is fundamentally the desire to be.

Thus the three categories "to be," "to make," and "to have" are reduced here as everywhere to two; "to make" is purely transitional. Ultimately a desire can be only the desire *to be* or the desire *to have*. On the other hand, it is seldom that play is pure of all appropriative tendency. I am passing over the desire of achieving a good performance or of beating a record, which can act as a stimulant for the sportsman; I am not even speaking of the desire "to have" a handsome body and harmonious muscles, which springs from the desire of appropriating objectively to myself my own being-for-others. These desires do not always enter in and besides they are not fundamental. But there is always in sport an appropriative component. In reality sport is a free transformation of the worldly environment into the supporting element of the action. This fact makes it creative like art. The environment may be a field of snow, an Alpine slope. To see it is already to possess it. In itself it is already apprehended by sight as a symbol of being.[5] It represents pure externality, radical spatiality; its indifferentiation, its monotony, and its whiteness manifest the absolute nudity of substance; it is the in-itself which is only in-itself, the being of the phenomenon, which being is manifested suddenly outside all phenomena. At the same time its *solid* immobility expresses the permanence and the objective resistance of the In-itself, its opaqueness and its impenetrability. Yet this first intuitive enjoyment can not suffice me. That pure in-itself, comparable to the absolute, intelligible plenum of Cartesian extension, fascinates me as the pure appearance of the not-self; what I wish precisely is that this in-itself might be like an emanation of myself while still remaining in itself. This is the meaning even of the snowmen and snowballs which children make; the goal is

[5] See Section 3.

to "make something out of snow"; that is, to impose on it a form which adheres so deeply to the matter that the matter appears to exist for the sake of the form. But if I approach, if I want to establish an appropriative contact with the field of snow, everything is changed. Its scale of being is modified; it exists bit by bit instead of existing in vast spaces; stains, brush, and crevices come to individualize each square inch. At the same time its solidity melts into water. I sink into the snow up to my knees; if I pick some up with my hands, it turns to liquid in my fingers; it runs off; there is nothing left of it. The in-itself is transformed into nothingness. My dream of appropriating the snow vanishes at the same moment. Moreover *I do not know what to do or what to make* with this snow which I have just come to see close at hand. I can not get hold of the field; I can not even reconstitute it as that substantial total which offered itself to my eyes and which has abruptly, doubly collapsed.

To ski means not only to enable me to make rapid movements and to acquire a technical skill, nor is it to *play* by increasing according to my whim the speed or difficulties of the course; it is also to enable me to *possess* this field of snow. At present *I am making something out of it.* That means that by my very activity as a skier, I am changing the matter and meaning of the snow. From the fact that now in my course it appears to me as a slope to go down, it finds again a continuity and a unity which it had lost. It is at the moment connective tissue. It is included between two limiting terms, it unites the point of departure with the point of arrival. Since in the descent I do not consider it in itself, bit by bit, but am always fixing on a point to be reached beyond the position which I now occupy, it does not collapse into an infinity of individual details but is *traversed toward* the point which I assign myself. This traversal is not only an activity of movement; it is also and especially a synthetic activity of organization and connection; I spread the skiing field before me in the same way that the geometrician, according to Kant, can apprehend a straight line only by drawing one. Furthermore this organization is marginal and not focal; it is not for itself and in itself that the field of snow is unified; the goal, posited and clearly perceived, the object of my attention is the spot at the edge of the field where I shall arrive. The snowy space is massed underneath implicitly; its cohesion is that of the blank space understood in the interior of a circumference, for example, when I look at the black line of the circle without paying explicit attention to its surface. And precisely because I maintain it marginal, implicit, and understood, it adapts itself to me, I have it well in hand; I pass beyond it toward its end just as a man hanging a tapestry passes beyond the hammer which he uses, toward its end, which is to nail an arras on the wall.

No appropriation can be more complete than this instrumental appropriation; the synthetic activity of appropriation is here a technical activity of utilization. The upsurge of the snow is the matter of my act in the same way that the upswing of the hammer is the pure fulfillment of the man hammering. At the same time I have chosen a certain point of view in order to apprehend this snowy slope: this point of view is a determined *speed*, which emanates from me, which I can increase or diminish as I like; through it the field traversed is constituted as a definite object, entirely distinct from what it would be at another speed. The speed organizes the ensembles at will; a specific object does or does not form a part of a particular group according to whether I have or have not taken a particular speed. (Think, for example, of Provence seen "on foot," "by car," "by train," "by bicycle." It offers as many different aspects according to whether or not Béziers is one hour, a morning's trip, or two days distant from Narbonne; that is, according to whether Narbonne is isolated and posited for itself with its environs or whether it constitutes a coherent group with Béziers and Sète, for example. In this last case Narbonne's *relation to the sea* is directly accessible to intuition; in the other it is denied; it can form the object only of a pure concept.) It is I myself then who give form to the field of snow by the free speed which I give myself. But at the same time I am acting upon *my matter*. The speed is not limited to imposing a form on a matter given from the outside; it *creates* its matter. The snow, which sank under my weight when I walked, which melted into water when I tried to pick it up, solidifies suddenly under the action of my speed; it supports me. It is not that I have lost sight of its lightness, its nonsubstantiality, its perpetual evanescence. Quite the contrary. It is precisely that lightness, that evanescence, that secret liquidity which hold me up; that is, which condense and melt in order to support me. That is because I hold a special relation of appropriation with the snow: *sliding*. This relation we will study later in detail. But at the moment we can grasp its essential meaning. We think of sliding as remaining on the surface. This is inexact; to be sure, I only skim the surface, and this skimming in itself is worth a whole study. Nevertheless I realize a synthesis which has depth. I realize that the bed of snow organizes itself in its lowest depths in order to hold me up; the sliding is

action *at a distance;* it assures my mastery
over the material without my needing to
plunge into that material and engulf myself
in it in order to overcome it. To slide is the
opposite of taking root. The root is already
half assimilated into the earth which nour-
ishes it; it is a living concretion of the earth;
it can utilize the earth only by making itself
earth; that is, by submitting itself, in a sense,
to the matter which it wishes to utilize. Sliding, on the contrary, realizes a material unity
in depth without penetrating farther than
the surface; it is like the dreaded master who
does not need to insist nor to raise his voice
in order to be obeyed. An admirable picture
of power. From this comes that famous ad-
vice: "Slide, mortals, don't bear down!" This
does not mean "Stay on the surface, don't go
deeply into things," but on the contrary,
"realize syntheses in depth without compromising yourselves."

Sliding is appropriation precisely because
the synthesis of support realized by the speed
is valid only for the slider and during the actual time when he is sliding. The solidity of
the snow is effective only for me, is sensible
only to me; it is a secret which the snow releases to me alone and which is already no
longer true *behind my back.* Sliding realizes
a strictly individual relation with matter, an
historical relation; the matter reassembles it-

self and solidifies in order to hold me up, and
it falls back exhausted and scattered behind
me. Thus by my passage I have realized that
which is unique *for me*. The ideal for sliding
then is a sliding which does not leave any
trace. It is sliding on water with a rowboat or
motor boat or especially with water skis
which, though recently invented, represent
from this point of view the ideal limit of
aquatic sports. Sliding on snow is already less
perfect; there is a trace behind me by which
I am compromised, however light it may be.
Sliding on ice, which scratches the ice and
finds a matter already organized, is very in-
ferior, and if people continue to do it despite
all this, it is for other reasons. Hence that
slight disappointment which always seizes us
when we see behind us the imprints which
our skis have left on the snow. How much better it would be if the snow reformed itself as
we passed over it! Besides when we let ourselves slide down the slope, we are accus-
tomed to the illusion of not making any
mark, we ask the snow to behave like that
water which secretly it is. Thus the sliding
appears as identical with a continuous creation. The speed is comparable to consciousness and here symbolizes consciousness.[6]
While it exists, it effects in the material the

[6] We have seen in Part Three the relation of movement
to the "for-itself".

birth of a deep quality which lives only so long as the speed exists, a sort of reassembling which conquers its indifferent externality and which falls back like a blade of grass behind the moving slider. The informing unification and synthetic condensation of the field of snow, which masses itself into an instrumental organization, which is *utilized,* like the hammer or the anvil, and which docilely adapts itself to an action which understands it and fulfills it; a continued and creative action on the very matter of the snow; the solidification of the *snowy mass* by the sliding; the similarity of the snow to the water which gives support, docile and without memory, or to the naked body of the woman, which the caress leaves intact and troubled in its inmost depths—such is the action of the skier on the real. But at the same time the snow remains impenetrable and out of reach; in one sense the action of the skier only develops its *potentialities.* It *makes it produce* what it can produce; the homogeneous, solid matter releases for him a solidity and homogeneity only through the act of the sportsman, but this solidity and this homogeneity dwell as properties enclosed in the matter. This synthesis of self and not-self which the sportsman's action here realizes is expressed, as in the case of speculative knowledge and the work of art, by the affirmation of the right of the skier over the snow. It is *my* field of snow; I have traversed it a hundred times, a hundred times I have through my speed effected the birth of this force of condensation and support; it is *mine*.

To this aspect of appropriation through sport, there must be added another—a difficulty overcome. It is more generally understood, and we shall scarcely insist on it here. Before descending this snowy slope, I must climb up it. And this ascent has offered to me another aspect of the snow-resistance. I have realized this resistance through my fatigue, and I have been able to measure at each instant the progress of my victory. Here the snow is identical with *the other,* and the common expressions "to overcome," "to conquer," "to master," *etc.* indicate sufficiently that it is a matter of establishing between me and the snow the relation of master to slave. This aspect of appropriation which we find in the ascent, exists also in swimming, in an obstacle course, *etc.* The peak on which a flag is planted is a peak which has been *appropriated.* Thus a principal aspect of sport—and in particular of open air sports—is the conquest of these enormous masses of water, of earth, and of air, which seem *a priori* indomitable and unutilizable; and in each case it is a question of possessing not the element for itself, but the type of existence in-itself which

is expressed through the instrumentality of
this element; it is the homogeneity of the substance which we wish to possess in the form
of snow; it is the impenetrability of the in-
itself and its non-temporal permanence which
we wish to appropriate in the form of the
earth or of the rock, *etc.* Art, science, play are
activities of appropriation, either wholly or
in part, and what they want to appropriate
beyond the concrete object of their quest is
being itself, the absolute being of the in-
itself.

Thus ontology teaches us that desire is originally a desire *of being* and that it is characterized as the free lack of being. But it
teaches us also that desire is a relation with a
concrete existent in the midst of the world
and that this existent is conceived as a type
of in-itself; it teaches us that the relation of
the for-itself to this desired in-itself is appropriation. We are, then, in the presence of a
double determination of desire: on the one
hand, desire is determined as a desire to be
a certain being, which is the *in-itself-for-itself*
and whose existence is ideal; on the other
hand, desire is determined in the vast majority of cases, as a relation with a contingent
and concrete in-itself, which it has the project
of appropriating.[7] Does one of these determi-

---

[7] Except where there is simply a *desire to be*—the desire
to be happy, to be strong, *etc.*

nations dominate the other? Are the two characteristics compatible? Existential psychoanalysis can be assured of its principles only if ontology has given a preliminary definition of the relation of these two beings—the concrete and contingent in-itself or object of the desire, and the in-itself-for-itself or ideal of the desire—and if it has made explicit the relation which unites appropriation as a type of relation to the in-itself, to being, as a type of relation to the in-itself-for-itself. This is what we must attempt at present.

What is meant by "to appropriate"? Or if you prefer, what do we understand by possessing an object? We have seen the reducibility of the category "to make," which allows us to see in it at one time "to be" and at another "to have." Is it the same with the category "to have"?

It is evident that in a great number of cases, to possess an object is to be able *to use it*. However, I am not satisfied with this definition. In this café I use this plate and this glass, yet they are not mine. I can not "use" that picture which hangs on my wall, and yet it *belongs to me*. The right which I have in certain cases to *destroy* what I possess is no more decisive. It would be purely abstract to define ownership by this right, and furthermore in a society with a "planned economy" an owner can possess his factory without hav-

ing the right to close it; in imperial Rome
the master possessed his slave but did not
have the right to put him to death. Besides
what is meant here by the *right* to destroy,
the right to use? I can see that this right refers
me to the social sphere and that ownership
seems to be defined within the compass of life
in society. But I see also that the right is
purely negative and is limited to preventing
another from destroying or using what belongs to me. Of course we could try to define
ownership as a social function. But first of all,
although society confers in fact the *right* to
possess according to certain rules, it does not
follow that it creates the relation of appropriation. At the very most it makes it legal. If
ownership is to be elevated to the rank of the
sacred, it must first of all exist as a relation
spontaneously established between the for-
itself and the concrete in-itself. If we can imagine the future existence of a more just
collective organization, where individual possession will cease to be protected and sanc-
tified at least within certain limits—this does
not mean that the appropriative tie will cease
to exist; it can remain indeed by virtue of a
private relation of men to things. Thus in
primitive societies where the matrimonial
bond is not yet a legal one and where hereditary descent is still matrilineal, the sexual tie
exists at the very least as a kind of concubi-

nage. It is necessary then to distinguish between possession and the right to possess. For
the same reason I must reject any definition
of the type which Proudhon gives—such as
"ownership is theft"—for it begs the question. It is possible of course for private property to be the *product* of theft and for the
holding of this property to have *for its result*
the robbing of another. But whatever may be
its origin and its results, ownership remains
no less capable of description and definition
in itself. The thief considers himself the
owner of the money which he has stolen. Our
problem then includes describing the precise
relation of the thief to the stolen goods as well
as the relation of the lawful owner to property "honestly acquired."

If I consider the object which I possess, I
see that the quality of *being possessed* does
not indicate a purely external denomination
marking the object's external relation to me;
on the contrary, this quality affects its very
depths; it appears to me and it appears to others as making a part of the object's being.
This is why primitive societies say of certain
individuals that they are "possessed"; the
"possessed" are thought of as *belonging* to
. . . This is also the significance of primitive
funeral ceremonies where the dead are buried with the objects which belong to them.
The rational explanation, "so that they can

use the objects," is evidently after the event. It is more probable that at the period when this kind of custom appeared spontaneously, no explanation seemed to be required. The objects had the specific quality *belonging to the deceased*. The formed a whole with him; there was no more question of burying the dead man without his usual objects than of burying him without one of his legs. The corpse, the cup from which the dead man drank, the knife which he used *make a single dead person*. The custom of burning widows in Malabar can very well be included under this principle; the woman has been possessed; the dead man takes her along with him in his death. In the eyes of the community, by rights she is dead; the burning is only to help her pass from this death by right to death in fact. Objects which can not be put in the grave are haunted. A ghost is only the concrete materialization of the idea that the house and furnishings "are possessed." To say that a house is haunted means that neither money nor effort will efface the metaphysical, absolute fact of *its possession* by a former occupant. It is true that the ghosts which haunt ancestral castles are degraded Lares. But what are these Lares if not layers of possession which have been deposited one by one on the walls and furnishings of the house? The very expression which designates the relation of the object to

its owner indicates sufficiently the deep penetration of the appropriation; to be possessed
means *to be for some one* (*être à* . . .). This
means that the possessed object is touched *in
its being*. We have seen moreover that the destruction of the possessor involves the destruction of the right of the possessed and inversely
the survival of the possessed involves the survival of the right of the possessor. The bond
of possession is an internal bond of *being*. I
meet the possessor in and through the object
which he possesses. This is evidently the explanation of the importance of *relics;* and we
mean by this not only religious relics, but
also and especially the totality of the property
of a famous man in which we try to rediscover
him, the souvenirs of the beloved dead which
seem to "perpetuate" his memory. (Consider,
for example, the Victor Hugo Museum, or
the "objects which belonged" to Balzac, to
Flaubert.)

This internal, ontological bond between
the possessed and the possessor (which cus-
toms like branding have often attempted to
materialize) can not be explained by a "realistic" theory of appropriation. If we are right
in defining realism as a doctrine which makes
subject and object two independent substances possessing existence for themselves
and by themselves, then a realistic theory can
no more account for appropriation than it

can for knowledge, which is one of the forms
of appropriation; both remain external relations uniting temporarily subject and object.
But we have seen that a substantial existence
must be attributed to the object known. It
is the same with ownership in general: the
possessed object exists in itself, is defined by
permanence, non-temporality, a sufficiency of
being, in a word by substantiality. Therefore we must put *Unselbstständigkeit* on the
side of the possessing subject. A substance
cannot appropriate another substance, and if
we apprehend in things a certain quality of
"being possessed," it is because originally the
internal relation of the for-itself to the in-
itself, which is ownership, derives its origin
from the insufficiency of being in the for-itself. It is obvious that the object possessed is
not *really* affected by the act of appropriation, any more than the object known is affected by knowledge. It remains untouched
(except in cases where the possessed is a human being, like a slave or a prostitute). But
this quality on the part of the possessed does
not affect its meaning ideally in the least; in
a word, its meaning is to reflect this possession
to the for-itself.

If the possessor and the possessed are
united by an internal relation based on the
insufficiency of being in the for-itself, we must
try to determine the nature and the meaning

EXISTENTIAL PSYCHOANALYSIS

of the *dyad,* which they form. In fact the internal relation is synthetic and effects the unification of the possessor and the possessed. This means that the possessor and the possessed constitute ideally a unique reality. To possess is to be united with the object possessed in the form of appropriation; to wish to possess is to wish to be united to an object in this relation. Thus the desire of a particular object is not the simple desire *of* this object; it is the desire to be united with the object in an internal relation, in the mode of constituting with it the unity "possessor-possessed." The desire *to have* is at bottom reducible to the desire to be related to a certain object in a certain *relation of being.*

In determining this relation, observations made earlier on the behaviour of the scientist, the artist, and the sportsman will be very useful to us. We discovered in the behaviour of each one a certain appropriative attitude, and the appropriation in each case was marked by the fact that the object appeared simultaneously to be a kind of subjective emanation of ourselves and yet to remain in an indifferently external relation with us. The "mine" appeared to us then as a relation of being intermediate between the absolute internality of the *me* and the absolute externality of the *not-me.* There is within the same syncretism a self becoming not-self and a not-self becoming self. But we must describe this relation more carefully. In the project of possession we meet a for-itself which is "*un-selbstständig*," separated by a nothingness from the possibility which it is. This possibility is the possibility of appropriating the *object*. We meet in addition a *value* which haunts the for-itself and which stands as the ideal indication of the total being which would be realized by the union in identity of the possibility and the for-itself which is its possibility; I mean here the being which would be realized if I were in the indissoluble unity of identity—myself and my property. Thus appropriation would be a relation of being between a for-itself and a concrete in-itself, and this relation would be pervaded by the ideal indication of an identification between this for-itself and the in-itself which is possessed.

To possess means *to have for myself;* that is, to be the proper end of the existence of the object. If possession is entirely and concretely given, the possessor is the reason for being (*raison d'être*) of the possessed object. I possess this pen; that means this pen exists *for me*, has been made *for me*. Moreover originally it is I who make for myself the object which I want to possess. My bow and arrows— that means the objects which I have made for myself. Division of labor can dim this original relation but cannot make it disappear. *Luxury* is a degradation of it; in the primitive form of luxury I possess an object which I *have had made* for myself by people belonging to *me* (slaves, servants born in the house). Luxury then is the form of ownership closest to primitive ownership; it is this which next to ownership itself throws the most light on the relation of *creation* which originally constitutes appropriation. This relation in a society where the division of labor is pushed to the limit, is hidden but not suppressed. The object which I possess is one which I *have bought*. Money represents my strength; it is less a possession in itself than an instrument for possessing. That is why except in most unusual cases of avarice, money is effaced before its possibility for purchase; it is evanescent, it is made to unveil the object, the concrete thing; money has only a transitive being. But *to me* it appears as a creative force: to buy an object is a symbolic act which amounts to creating the object. That is why money is synonymous with power; not only because it is in fact capable of procuring for us what we desire, but especially because it represents the effectiveness of my desire as such. Precisely because it is transcended toward the thing, surpassed, and simply *implied,* it represents my magical bond with the object. Money suppresses the *technical* connec-

tion of subject and object and renders the
desire immediately operative, like the magic
wishes of fairy tales. Stop before a show case
with money in your pocket; the objects dis-
played are already more than half yours.
Thus money establishes a bond of appropriation between the for-itself and the total collection of objects in the world. By means of
money desire as such is already informer and
creator.

Thus through a continuous degradation,
the bond of creation is maintained between
subject and object. To have is first to create.
And the bond of ownership which is established then is a bond of continuous creation;
the object possessed is inserted by me into the
total form of *my* environment; its existence is
determined by my situation and by its inte-
gration in that same situation. *My* lamp is
not only that electric bulb, that shade, that
wrought iron stand; it is a certain power of
lighting *this* desk, these books, this table; it
is a certain luminous nuance of my work at
night in connection with my habits of reading
or writing late; it is animated, colored, defined by the use which I make of it; *it is* that
use and exists only through it. If isolated
from my desk, from my work, and placed in
a lot of objects on the floor of a salesroom, my
lamp is radically extinguished; it is no longer
my lamp; instead merely a member of the

class of lamps, it has returned to its original matter. Thus I am responsible for the existence of my possessions in the human order. Through ownership I raise them up to a certain type of functional being; and my simple *life* appears to me as creative exactly because by its continuity it perpetuates the quality of *being possessed* in each of the objects in my possession. I draw the collection of my surroundings into being along with myself. If they are taken from me, they die as my arm would die if it were severed from me.

But the original, radical relation of creation is a relation of emanation, and the difficulties encountered by the Cartesian theory of substance are there to help us discover this relation. What I create is mine—if by creating we mean to bring matter and form to existence. The tragedy of the absolute Creator, if he existed, would be the impossibility of getting out of himself, for whatever he created could be only himself. Where could my creation derive any objectivity and independence since its form and its matter are from me? Only a sort of inertia could close it off from my presence, but in order for this same inertia to function, I must sustain it in existence by a continuous creation. Thus to the extent that I appear to myself as *creating* objects by the sole relation of appropriation, these objects are *myself*. The totality of my possessions reflects the totality of my being. I *am* what I have. It is I myself which I touch in this cup, in this trinket. This mountain which I climb is myself to the extent that I conquer it; and when I am at its summit, which I have "achieved" at the cost of this same effort, when I attain this magnificent view of the valley and the surrounding peaks, then I *am* the view; the panorama is myself dilated to the horizon, for it exists only through me, only for me. But creation is an evanescent concept which can exist only through its movement. If we stop it, it disappears. At the extreme limits of its acceptance, it is annihilated; either I find only my pure subjectivity or else I encounter a naked, indifferent materiality which no longer has any relation to me. *Creation* can be conceived and maintained only as a continued transition from one term to the other. As the object rises up in my world, it must simultaneously be wholly me and wholly independent of me. This is what we believe that we are realizing in possession. The possessed object as possessed is a continuous creation; but still it remains there, it exists by itself; it is in-itself; if I turn away from it, it does not thereby cease to exist; if I go away, it *represents* me in my desk, in my room, in *this* place in the world. From the start it is impenetrable. This pen is entirely myself, at the very point at which I no longer even distinguish it from the act of writing, which is *my* act. And yet, on the other hand, it is intact; my ownership does not change it; there is only an ideal relation between it and me. In a sense I enjoy my ownership if I surpass it toward use, but if I wish to contemplate it, the bond of possession is effaced, I no longer understand what it means to possess. The pipe there on the table is independent, indifferent. I pick it up, I feel it, I contemplate it so as to realize this appropriation; but just because these gestures are meant to give me the *enjoyment* of this appropriation, they miss their mark. I have merely an inert, wooden stem between my fingers. It is only when I pass beyond *my* objects toward a goal, when I utilize them, that I can enjoy their possession.

Thus the relation of continuous creation incloses within it as its implicit contradiction the absolute independence, the in-itself of the objects created. Possession is a magical relation; I *am* these objects which I possess, but outside, so-to-speak, facing myself; I create them as independent of me; what I possess is mine outside of me, outside all subjectivity, as an in-itself which escapes me at each instant and whose creation at each instant I perpetuate. But precisely because I am always somewhere outside of myself, as an incompleteness which makes its being known by what it is not, now when I possess, I transfer myself to the object possessed; without it I am nothing save a nothingness which possesses, nothing other than pure and simple possession, an incompleteness, an insufficiency, whose sufficiency and completion are there in that object. In possession, I am my own foundation in so far as I exist in an in-itself; in so far as possession is a continuous creation, I apprehend the possessed object as established by me in its being; on the other hand, in so far as creation is emanation, this object is reabsorbed in me, it is only myself; finally, in so far as it is originally in itself, it is not-me, it is myself facing myself, objective, in itself, permanent, impenetrable, existing in relation to me in the relation of externality, of indifference. Thus I am the foundation for myself in so far as I exist as an indifferent in-itself in relation to myself. But this is precisely the project of the in-itself-for-itself. For this ideal being is defined as an in-itself which, as for-itself, would be its own foundation, or as a for-itself whose original project would not be a mode of being but a being, precisely the being-in-itself which it is. We see the appropriation is nothing save the *symbol* of the ideal of the for-itself or value. The dyad for-itself possessing and in-itself possessed is the same as that being which exists in order to possess itself and whose possession is its own creation—God. Thus the possessor aims at enjoying being-in-itself, his being-outside. Through possession I recover an object-being identical with my being-for-others. Consequently the other can not surprise me; the being which he wishes to bring into the world which is myself-for-another—this being I already enjoy possessing. Thus possession is in addition a *defense against others*. What is mine is myself in a non-subjective form inasmuch as I am its free foundation.

We can not insist too strongly on the fact that this relation is *symbolic* and *ideal*. My original desire of being my own foundation for myself is never satisfied through appropriation any more than Freud's patient satisfies his Oedipus complex when he dreams that a soldier kills the Czar (i.e., his father). This is why ownership appears to the owner simultaneously as something given at a particular instant in the eternal and as requiring an infinite time to be realized. No particular act of utilization really realizes the enjoyment of full possession; but it refers to other appropriative acts, each one of which has the value of an incantation. To possess a bicycle is to be able first to look at it, then to touch it. But touching is revealed as being insufficient; what is necessary is to be able to get on the bicycle and take a ride. But this *gratuitous* ride is likewise insufficient; it would be necessary to use the bicycle to go on some errands. And this refers us to longer uses and more complete, to long trips across France. But these trips themselves disintegrate into a thousand appropriative behaviour patterns, each one of which refers to others. Finally as one could foresee, handing over a bank-note is enough to make the bicycle belong to me, but my entire life is needed to realize this possession. In acquiring the object, I perceive that possession is an enterprise which death always renders still unachieved. Now we can understand why; it is because it is impossible to realize the relation symbolized by appropriation. In itself appropriation contains nothing concrete. It is not a real activity (such as eating, drinking, sleeping) which could serve in addition as a symbol for a particular desire. It exists, on the contrary, only by virtue of a symbol; it is its symbolism which gives it its meaning, its coherence, its existence. There can be found in it no positive enjoyment outside its symbolic value; it is only the indication of a supreme enjoyment of possession (that of the being which would be the foundation for itself), which is always beyond all the appropriative behaviour patterns meant to realize it.

This is precisely why the recognition that it is impossible to *possess* an object involves

or the for-itself a violent urge to *destroy* it.
To destroy is to reabsorb into myself; it is to
enter along with the being-in-itself of the
destroyed object into a relation as profound
as that of creation. The flames which burn the
farm which I myself have set on fire, gradu-
ally effect the fusion of the farm with myself.
In annihilating it I am changing it into *myself*. Suddenly I rediscover the relation of
being found in creation, but in reverse; I
am the foundation of the barn which is burning; *I am* this barn since I am destroying its
being. Destruction realizes appropriation perhaps more keenly than creation does, for
the object destroyed is no longer there to
show itself impenetrable. It has the impenetrability and the sufficiency of being of the in-
itself which it *has been,* but at the same time
it has the invisibility and translucency of the
nothingness which I am, since it *no longer
exists.* This glass which I have broken and
which "was" on this table, is there still, but
as an absolute transparency. I see all beings
superimposed. This is what movie producers
have attempted to render by overprinting the
film. The destroyed object resembles a consciousness although it has the irreparability of
the in-itself. At the same time it is positively
mine because the mere fact that I have to
maintain my own continuity keeps the destroyed object from being annihilated. I re-

create it by recreating myself; thus to destroy is to recreate by assuming oneself as solely responsible for the being of what existed *for all*.

Destruction then is to be given a place among appropriative behaviours. Moreover many kinds of appropriative conduct have a destructive structure along with others. To utilize is to use. In *making use* of my bicycle, I *use it up*—wear it out; that is, continuous appropriative creation is marked by a partial destruction. This wear can cause distress for strictly practical reasons, but in the majority of cases it brings a secret joy, almost like the joy of possession; this is because it is coming from us—we are consuming. It should be noted that the word "consume" holds the double meaning of an appropriative destruction and an alimentary enjoyment. To consume is to annihilate and it is to eat; it is to destroy by incorporating into oneself. If I ride on my bicycle, I can be annoyed at wearing out its tires because it is difficult to find others to replace them; but the image of enjoyment which my body invokes is that of a destructive appropriation, of a "creation-destruction." The bicycle gliding alone, carrying me, by its very movement is created and made mine; but this creation is deeply impressed into the object by the light, continued wear which is impressed on it and which is like the brand on the slave. The object is mine because it is I who have used it; the using up of what is mine is the obverse of *my* life.[8]

These remarks will enable us to understand better the meaning of certain feelings or behaviour ordinarily considered as irreducible; for example, *generosity.* Actually the *gift* is a primitive form of destruction. We know for example that the potlatch involves the destruction of enormous quantities of merchandise. These destructions are forbidden to the other; the gifts enchain him. On this level it is indifferent whether the object is destroyed or given to another; in any case the potlatch is destruction and enslavement of the other. I destroy the object by giving it away as well as by annihilating it; I suppress in it the quality of being *mine,* which constituted it to the depths of its being; I remove it from my sight; I constitute it—in relation to my table, to my room—as *absent;* I alone shall preserve for it the ghostly, transparent being of *past* objects, because I am the one through whom beings pursue an honorary existence after their annihilation. Thus generosity is above all a destructive function. The craze for giving which sometimes seizes certain people is first and foremost a craze to de-

[8] Brummell carried his elegance to the extent of wearing only clothes which had been worn a little. He had a horror of anything new; what is new is "dressed up" because it does not belong to anybody.

stroy; it is equivalent to an attitude of mad-
ness, a "love" which accompanies the shat-
tering of objects. But the craze to destroy
which is at the bottom of generosity is nothing else than a craze to possess. All which I
abandon, all which I give, I enjoy in a
higher manner through the fact that I give
it away; giving is a keen, brief enjoyment, almost sexual. To give is to enjoy possessively
the object which one gives; it is a destructive-
appropriative contact. But at the same time
the gift casts a spell over the recipient; it
obliges him to recreate, to maintain in being by a continuous creation this bit of myself
which I no longer want, which I have just
possessed up to its annihilation, and which
finally remains only as an image. To give is
to enslave. That aspect of the gift does not
interest us here, for it concerns primarily our
relations with others. What we wish to em-
phasize is that generosity is not irreducible;
to give is to appropriate by destruction while
utilizing this destruction to enslave another.
Generosity then is a feeling structured by the
existence of another and indicates a preference for *appropriation by destruction*. In
this way it leads us toward *nothingness* still
more than toward the in-itself (we have here
a nothingness of in-itself which is evidently
itself in-itself but which as nothingness can
symbolize with the being which is its own

nothingness) . If then existential psychoanalysis encounters evidence of *generosity* in a
subject, it must search further for his original project and ask why the subject has chosen to appropriate by destruction rather than
by creation. The answer to this question will
discover that original relation to being which
constitutes the *person* who is being studied.

These observations aim only at bringing to
light the *ideal* character of the appropriative
tie and the symbolic function of all appropriative conduct. It is necessary to add that the
symbol is not deciphered by the subject himself. It has not been prepared by a symbolic
process in an unconscious but comes from the
very structure of being-in-the-world. We have
seen in the chapter devoted to transcendence that the order of instruments in the
world is the result of my projecting into the
in-itself the image of my possibilities—that is,
of what I am—but that I could never decipher this worldly image since it would require nothing less than reflective schizogene-
sis to enable me to consider myself in the
pattern of an object. Thus since the circuit
of selfness is non-thetic and consequently the
identification of what I am remains non-the-
matic,[9] this "being-in-itself" of myself which
the world refers to as me is necessarily hidden
from my *knowledge*. I can only adapt my-

[9] *I.e.*, with no subject and no object.

self to it in and through the approximative action which gives it birth. Consequently to possess does not mean to know that one holds with the object possessed a relation identified as creation-destruction; rather to possess means *to be in this relation* or better yet *to be this relation.* The possessed object has for us an immediately apprehensible quality which transforms it entirely—the quality of being *mine*—but this quality is in itself strictly undecipherable; it reveals itself in and through action. It makes clear that it has a particular meaning, but from the moment that we want to withdraw a little in relation to the object and to contemplate it, the quality vanishes without revealing its deeper structure and its meaning. This withdrawal indeed is itself destructive of the appropriative connection. An instant earlier I was engaged in an ideal totality, and precisely because I was engaged in my being, I could not know it; an instant later the totality has been broken and I can not discover the meaning of it in the disconnected fragments which formerly composed it. This can be observed in that contemplative experience called depersonalization which certain patients have in spite of efforts to resist it. We are forced then to have recourse to existential psychoanalysis to reveal in each particular case the meaning of the appropriative synthesis for which we have just determined the general, abstract meaning by ontology.

It remains to determine in general the meaning of the object possessed. This investigation should complete our knowledge of the appropriative project. What then is it which we seek to appropriate?

In the first place it is easy to see abstractly that we originally aim at possessing not so much the mode of being of an object as the actual being of this particular object. In fact it is as a representative of being-in-itself that I desire to appropriate it; that is, to apprehend that ideally I am the foundation of its being in so far as it is a part of myself and on the other hand to apprehend that empirically the appropriated object is never valid in itself alone nor in its individual use. No particular appropriation has any meaning outside its indefinite extensions: the pen which I possess is the same as all other pens; it is the class of pens which I possess in it. But in addition I possess in it the possibility of writing, of tracing with certain characteristic forms and color (for I combine the instrument itself and the ink which I use in it). These characteristic forms and color with their meaning are condensed in the pen as well as the paper, its special resistance, its odor, *etc.* With *all* possession there is made the crystallizing synthesis which Stendhal has described for the one case of love. Each possessed object which lifts itself on the foundation of the world, manifests the entire world, just as a beloved woman manifests the sky, the shore, the sea which surrounded her when she appeared. To appropriate this object is then to appropriate the world symbolically. Each one can recognize it by referring to his own experience: for myself, I shall cite a personal example, not to prove the point but to guide the reader in his inquiry.

Some years ago I brought myself to the decision not to smoke any more. The struggle was hard, and in truth, I did not care so much for the *taste* of the tobacco which I was going to lose, as for the *meaning* of the act of smoking. A complete crystallization had been formed. I used to smoke at the theater, in the morning while working, in the evening after dinner, and it seemed to me that in giving up smoking I was going to strip the theater of its interest, the evening meal of its savor, the morning work of its fresh animation. Whatever unexpected happening was going to meet my eye, it seemed to me that it was fundamentally impoverished from the moment that I could not welcome it while smoking. To-be-capable-of-being-met-by-me-smoking: such was the concrete quality which had been spread over everything. It seemed to me that I was going to snatch it away from everything and that in the midst of this universal impoverishment, life was scarcely worth the effort. But to smoke is an appropriative, destructive action. Tobacco is a symbol of "appropriated" being, since it is destroyed in the rhythm of my breathing, in a mode of "continuous destruction," since it passes into me and its change in myself is manifested symbolically by the transformation of the consumed solid into smoke. The connection between the landscape seen while I was smoking and this little crematory sacrifice was such that as we have just seen, the the tobacco symbolized the landscape. This means then that the act of destructively appropriating the tobacco was the symbolic equivalent of destructively appropriating the entire world. Across the tobacoo which I was smoking was the world which was burning, which was going up in smoke, which was being reabsorbed into vapor so as to re-enter into me. In order to maintain my decision not to smoke, I had to realize a sort of decrystallization; that is, without exactly accounting to myself for what I was doing, I reduced the tobacco to being nothing but itself—an herb which burns. I cut its symbolic ties with the world; I persuaded myself that I was not taking anything away from the play at the theater, from the landscape, from the book which I was reading, if I considered them without my pipe; that is, I rebuilt my possession of these objects in modes other than that sacrificial ceremony. As soon as I was persuaded of this, my regret was reduced to a very small matter; I deplored the thought of not perceiving the odor of the smoke, the warmth of the bowl between my fingers and so forth. But suddenly my regret was disarmed and quite bearable.

Thus what fundamentally we desire to appropriate in an object is its being and it is the world. These two ends of appropriation are in reality only one. I search behind the phenomenon to possess the being of the phenomenon. But this being, as we have seen, is very different from the phenomenon of being; it is being-in-itself, and not only the being of a particular thing. It is not because there is here a passage to the universal but rather the being considered in its concrete nudity becomes suddenly the being of the totality. Thus the relation of possession appears to us clearly: to possess is to wish to possess the world through a particular object. And as possession is defined as the effort to apprehend ourselves as the foundation of a being in so far as it is ourselves ideally, every possessive project aims at constituting the For-itself as the foundation of the world or a concrete totality of the in-itself, and this totality is, as totality, the for-itself which exists in the mode of the in-itself. To-be-in-the-world is to form the project of possessing the world; that is, to apprehend the total world as that which is lacking to the for-itself in order that it may become in-itself-for-itself. It is to be engaged in a totality which is precisely the ideal or value or totalized totality and which would be ideally constituted by the fusion of the for-itself, as a detotalized totality which has to be what it is, with the world, as the totality of the in-itself which is what it is. It must be understood of course that the project of the for-itself is not to establish a being of reason, that is a being which the for-itself would first conceive—form and matter—and then cause to exist. Such a being actually would be a pure abstraction, a universal; its conception could not be prior to being-in-the-world; on the contrary its conception would presuppose being-in-the-world as it supposes the preontological comprehension of a being which is eminently concrete and present at the start, which is the "there" of the first being-there of the for-itself; that is, the being of the world. The for-itself does not first think a universal and then determine itself in the function of concepts. It is its choice and its choice can not be abstract without making the very being of the for-itself abstract. The being of the for-itself is an individual venture, and the choice must be an individual choice of a concrete being.

This applies, as we have seen, to *situation* in general. The choice of the for-itself is always a choice of a concrete situation in its incomparable uniqueness. But it is true as well for the ontological meaning of this choice. When we say that the for-itself is a project of *being*, we do not mean that the being-in-itself which it forms the project of being, is conceived by the for-itself as a structure common to all existents of a certain type; its project is in no way a conception, as we have seen. That which it forms the project of being appears to it as an eminently concrete totality; it is *this* particular being. Of course we can foresee in this project the possibilities of a universalizing development; but it is in the same way as we say of a lover that he loves all women or all womankind in one woman. The for-itself has the project of being the foundation of this concrete being, which as we have just seen, can not be *conceived*—for the very reason that it is concrete; neither can it be imagined, for the imaginary is nothingness and this being is eminently being. It must *exist;* that is, it must be encountered, but this encounter is identical with the choice which the for-itself makes. The for-itself is an encountered-choice; that is, it is defined as a choice of establishing the being which it encounters. That means that the for-itself as an individual enterprise is a choice of *this world,* as a totality of individual being; it does not surpass it towards a logical universal but towards a new concrete "state" in the same world, in which the being would be an in-itself established by the for-itself; that is, it surpasses it towards a concrete-being-beyond-the-concrete-existing-being. Thus being-in-the-world is a project of possessing this world and the value which haunts the for-itself is the concrete indication of an individual being constituted by the synthetic function of *this* for-itself and *this* world. Being, in fact, whatever it may be, wherever it may come from, and in whatever mode we may consider it, whether it is in-itself or for-itself or the impossible ideal of in-itself-for-itself, remains in its original contingency an individual venture.

Now we can define the relations which unite the two categories, *to be* and *to have*. We have seen that desire can be originally either the desire to be or the desire to have. But the desire to have is not irreducible. While the desire to be bears directly on the for-itself and has the project of conferring on it without intermediary the dignity of in-itself-for-itself, the desire to have aims at the for-itself on, in, and through the world. It is by the appropriation of the world that the project to have aims at realizing the same value as the desire to be. That is why these desires, which can be distinguished by analysis, are in reality inseparable. It is impossible to find a desire to be which is not accompanied by a desire to have, and conversely. Fundamentally we have to deal with two ways of looking toward a single goal, or if you prefer, with two interpretations of the same fundamental situation, the one tending to confer being on the For-itself without detour, the other establishing the circuit of selfness; that is, inserting the world between the for-itself and its being. As for the original situation, it is the lack of being which I am; that is, which I make myself be. But the being of which I make myself a lack is strictly individual and concrete; it is the being which *exists already* and in the midst of which I arise as being *its* lack. Thus the very nothingness which I am is individual and concrete, as being *this* annihilation and not any other.

Every for-itself is a free choice; each of its acts—the most insignificant as well as the most weighty—expresses this choice and emanates from it. This is what we have called our freedom. We have now grasped the *meaning* of this choice; it is a choice of being, either directly or by the appropriation of the world, or rather by both at once. Thus my freedom is a choice of being God and all my acts, all my projects translate this choice and reflect it in a thousand and one modes, for there is an infinity of modes of being and of

modes of having. The goal of existential psychoanalysis is to rediscover through these
empirical, concrete projects the original mode
in which each man has chosen his being. It
remains to explain, someone will say, why I
choose to possess the world through *this* particular object rather than another. We shall
reply that here we see the peculiar character
of freedom.

Yet the object itself is not irreducible. In it
we aim at its *being* through its mode of being
or quality. Quality—particularly a material
quality like the fluidity of water or the
density of a stone,—is a mode of being and so
can only present being in one certain way.
What we choose is a certain way in which being discovers itself and lets itself be possessed.
The yellow and red, the taste of a tomato, or
the wrinkled softness of split peas are by no
means irreducible data according to our view.
They translate symbolically to our perception a certain way which being has of giving
itself, and we react by disgust or desire, according to how we see being spring forth in
one way or another from their surface. Existential psychoanalysis must bring out the *ontological meaning* of qualities. It is only thus
—and not by considerations of sexuality—
that we can explain, for example, certain con-
stants in poetic "imaginations" (Rimbaud's
"geological," Poe's fluidity of water) or sim-

ply the *tastes* of each one, those famous tastes which we are forbidden to discuss without taking into account that they symbolize in their own way a whole *"Weltanschauung,"* a whole choice of being and that hence comes their *self-evidence* to the eyes of the man who has made them his. Our next procedure then is to sketch in outline this particular attempt of existential psychoanalysis, for the sake of making suggestions for further research. For it is not on the level of a taste for sweetness or for bitterness and the like that the free choice is irreducible but on the level of the choice of the aspect of being which is revealed through and by means of sweetness, bitterness, and the rest.

III

QUALITY AS A REVELATION OF BEING

WHAT WE must do is to attempt a psychoanalysis of *things*. M. Bachelard has tried this and shown much talent in his last book, *Water and Dreams*. There is great promise in this work; in particular the author has made a real discovery in his "material imagination." Yet in truth this term *imagination* does not suit us and neither does that attempt to look behind things and their gelatinous, solid, or fluid matter, for the "images" which we project there. Perception, as I have shown elsewhere,[1] has nothing in common with imagination; on the contrary each rigorously excludes the other. To perceive does not mean to assemble images by means of sensations; this thesis, originating with the association theory in psychology, must be banished entirely. Consequently psychoanalysis will not look for images but rather will seek to explain the meaning which really belongs to

[1] *L'Imaginaire.* N.R.F., 1939.

things. Of course the "human" meaning of *sticky,* of *slimy, etc.* does not belong to the in-itself. But potentialities do not belong to it either, as we have seen, and yet it is these which constitute the world. The meaning of matter, the human sense of needles, snow, grained wood, of crowded, of greasy, *etc.,* are as real as the world, neither more nor less, and to come into the world means to become familiar with these meanings. But no doubt we have to do here with a simple difference in terminology. M. Bachelard appears bolder and seems to expose the basis of his thought when he speaks in his studies of psychoanalyzing plants or when he entitles one of his works *The Psychoanalysis of Fire.* Actually he is applying not *to the subject* but to things a method of objective interpretation which does not suppose any previous reference to the subject. When for instance I wish to determine the objective meaning of snow, I see, for example, that it melts at certain temperatures and that this melting of the snow is its death. Here we merely have to do with objective confirmation. When I wish to determine the meaning of this melting, I must compare it to other objects located in other regions of existence but equally objective, equally transcendent—ideas, friendship, persons—concerning which I can also say that they melt. Money *melts* in my hands. I am

swimming and I *melt* in the water. Certain
ideas—in the sense of socially objective meanings—"snowball" and others *melt* away. We
say, "How thin he has become! How he has
melted away!" (*Comme il a fondu!*)² Doubtless I shall thus obtain a certain relation
binding certain forms of being to certain
others.

It is important to compare the melting
snow to certain other more mysterious examples of melting. Take for example the content of certain old myths. The tailor in
Grimm's fairy tales takes a piece of cheese in
his hands, pretends it is a stone, squeezes it so
hard that the whey oozes out of it; his as-
sistants believe that he has made a stone drip,
that he is extracting the liquid from it. Such
a comparison informs us of a secret liquid
quality in solids, in the sense in which Audi-
berti by a happy inspiration spoke of the
secret blackness of milk. This liquidity which
ought to be compared to the juice of fruits and
to human blood—which is to man something
like his own secret liquidity—this liquidity
refers us to a certain permanent possibility
which the "granular compact" (designating
a certain quality of the being of the *pure
in-itself*) possesses of changing itself into *ho-
mogenous, undifferentiated fluidity* (another
quality of the being of the pure in-itself).

² We may recall also the "melting money" of Daladier.

We apprehend here in its origin and with all its ontological signification, the polarity of the continuous and discontinuous, the feminine and masculine poles of the world, for which we shall subsequently see the dialectical development all the way to the quantum theory and wave mechanics. Thus we shall succeed in deciphering the secret meaning of the snow, which is an ontological meaning.

But in all this where is the relation to the subjective? To imagination? All we have done is to compare strictly objective structures and to formulate the hypothesis which can unify and group these structures. That is why psychoanalysis depends here on the things themselves, not upon men. That is also why I should have less confidence than M. Bachelard in resorting at this level to the material imaginations of poets, whether Lautréamont, Rimbaud, or Poe. To be sure, it is fascinating to look for the "Bestiary of Lautréamont." But actually if in this research we have returned to the subjective, we shall attain results truly significant only if we consider Lautréamont as an original and pure preference for animality, and if we have first determined the objective meaning of animality.[3] In fact if Lautréamont *is what he prefers,* it is necessary first to understand the nature of what he

[3] One aspect of this animality is exactly what Scheler calls *vital values.*

prefers. To be sure, we know well what he is going "to put" into the animal world, something different and more than I put into it. But the subjective enrichments which inform us about Lautréamont are polarized by the objective structure of animality. This is why the existential psychoanalysis of Lautréamont supposes first an interpretation of the objective meaning of *animal*. Similarly I have thought for a long time of establishing a *lapidary* for Rimbaud. But what meaning would it have unless we had previously established the significance of geology in general?

It will be objected that a meaning presupposes man. We do not deny this. But man, being transcendence, establishes the meaningful by his very coming into the world and the meaningful because the very structure of transcendence is a reference to other transcendents which can be interpreted without recourse to the subjectivity which has established it. The potential energy of a body is an objective quality of that body which can be objectively calculated while taking into account unique objective circumstances. And yet this energy can come to dwell in a body only in a world whose appearance is a correlative of that of a for-itself. Similarly a rigorously objective psychoanalysis will discover that deeply engaged in the matter of things there are other potentialities which remain

entirely transcendent even though they cor-
respond to a still more fundamental choice
of human reality, a choice of *being*.

That brings us to the second point in which
we differ with M. Bachelard. Certainly any
psychoanalysis must have its principles *a
priori*. In particular it must know *what it is
looking for,* or how will it be able to find it?
But since the end of its research can not itself
be established by the psychoanalysis, without
falling into a vicious circle, such end must be
the object of a postulate; either we seek it in
experience, or we establish it by means of
some other discipline. The Freudian libido is
obviously a simple postulate; Adler's will to
power seems to be an unmethodical generali-
zation from empirical data—and in fact it is
this very lack of method which allows him to
disregard the basic principles of a psychoanalytic method. M. Bachelard seems to rely
upon these predecessors; the postulate of sexuality seems to dominate his research; at
other times we are referred to *Death,* to the
trauma of birth, to the will to power. In short
his psychoanalysis seems more sure of its
method than of its principles and doubtless
will count on its results to enlighten it concerning the precise goal of its research. But
this is to put the cart before the horse; consequences will never allow us to establish the
principle, any more than the summation of

finite modes will permit us to apprehend substance. It appears to us then that we must here
abandon these empirical principles or these
postulates which would make man *a priori* a
sexuality or a will to power, and that we
should establish the goal of psychoanalysis
strictly in terms of ontology. This is what we
have just attempted. We have seen that human reality, far from being capable of being
described as *libido* or will to power, is a
choice of being, either directly or through appropriation of the world. And we have seen
—when the choice is expressed through appropriation—that each *thing* is chosen in the
last analysis, not for its sexual potential but
depending on the mode in which it renders
being, depending on the manner in which
being springs forth from its surface. A psychoanalysis of *things* and of their *matter* ought
above all to be concerned with establishing
the way in which each thing is the *objective*
symbol of being and of the relation of human
reality to this being. We do not deny that we
should discover afterwards a whole sexual
symbolism in nature, but it is a secondary and
reducible stratum, which supposes first a psychoanalysis of presexual structures. Thus M.
Bachelard's study of water, which abounds in
ingenious and profound insights, will be for
us a set of suggestions, a precious collection
of materials which should now be utilized by

a psychoanalysis which is aware of its own principles.

What ontology can teach psychoanalysis is first of all the *true* origin of the meanings of things and their *true* relation to human reality. Ontology alone in fact can take its place on the plane of transcendence and from a single viewpoint apprehend being-in-the-world in both its aspects, because ontology alone has its place originally in the perspective of the *cogito*. Once again the ideas of facticity and situation will enable us to understand the existential symbolism of things. We have seen that it is in theory possible but in practice impossible to distinguish facticity from the project which constitutes it in situation. This fact can be of use to us here; we have seen that there is no necessity to hold that the "this" of an object has any meaning whatever when considered in the indifferent externality of its being and independently from the upsurge of the for-itself. Actually its quality, as we have seen, is nothing other than its being. The yellow of the lemon, we said, is not a subjective mode of apprehending the lemon; it *is the lemon*. We have shown also that the whole lemon extends throughout its qualities and that each one of the qualities is spread over the others; that is what we have correctly called "this." [4] Every quality of be-

---

[4] Part Two, ch. III, section 3.

ing is all of being; it is the presence of its absolute contingency; it is its indifferent irreducibility. Yet in Part Two we insisted on the
inseparability of project and facticity in the
single quality. "For a quality to exist, it is necessary that there exist a being for a nothingness which by nature is not the being . . .
Quality is being unveiling itself completely
within the limitations of the *there is*." Thus
from the beginning we could not attribute the
meaning of a quality to being *in-itself,* since
the "there is" is already necessary; that is, the
annihilating mediation of the for-itself must
be there in order for qualities to be there.
But it is easy to understand in view of these
remarks that the meaing of quality in turn indicates something as a reenforcement of the
"there is," since we take it as our support in
order to surpass the "there is" toward being
as it is absolutely and in-itself. In each apprehension of quality, there is in this sense a
metaphysical effort to escape from our condition so as to pierce through the casing of
nothingness about the "there is" and to pene-
trate to the pure in-itself. But obviously we
can apprehend quality only as a symbol of a
being which totally escapes us, even though it
is totally there before us; in short, we can only
make revealed being function as a symbol of
being in-itself. This means that a new structure of the "there is" is constituted which is

126 EXISTENTIAL PSYCHOANALYSIS

the meaningful level although this level is revealed in the absolute unity of one and the
same fundamental project. This structure we
shall call the metaphysical term of all revelation intuitive of being; and this is precisely
what we ought to achieve and disclose by psychoanalysis. What is the metaphysical term of
yellow, of red, of polished, of wrinkled? And
after these elementary questions, what is the
metaphysical coefficient of lemon, of water,
of oil, *etc.?* Psychoanalysis must resolve all
these problems if it wants to understand some-
day why Pierre likes oranges and has a horror
of water, why he gladly eats tomatoes and refuses to eat beans, why he vomits if he is
forced to swallow oysters or raw eggs.

We have shown also, however, the error
which we would make by believing that we
"project" our affective inclinations on the
thing, to illuminate it or color it. First, as was
seen early in the discussion, a feeling is not
an inner disposition but an objective, tran-
scending relation which has as its object to
learn what it is. But this is not all. The explanation by projection, which is found in such
trite sayings as "A landscape is a spiritual
state," always begs the question. Take for example that particular quality which we call
slimy.[5] Certainly for the European adult it

[5] French *visqueux*. This at times comes closer to the
English "sticky", but I have consistently used the word

signifies a host of *human* and *moral* characteristics which can easily be reduced to relations of being. A handshake, a smile, a
thought, a feeling can be slimy. The common
opinion is that first I have experienced certain
behaviour and certain moral attitudes which
displease me and which I condemn; and that,
in addition, I have a sensory intuition of
"slimy." Afterwards, says the theory, I should
establish a connection between these feelings
and sliminess and the slimy would function
as a symbol of a whole class of human feelings
and attitudes. I would then have enriched the
slimy by projecting upon it my knowledge of
that human category of behaviour.

But how are we to accept this explanation
by projection? If we suppose that we have
first apprehended the feelings as pure psychic qualities, how will we be able to apprehend their relation to the slimy? A feeling
apprehended in its qualitative purity will be
able to reveal itself only as a certain purely
unextended disposition, culpable because of
its relation to certain values and certain consequences; in any case it will not "form an
image" unless the image has been given first.
On the other hand if "slimy" is not originally
charged with an affective meaning, if it is
given only as a certain material quality, one

"slimy" in translating because the figurative meaning of
"slimy" appears to be identical in both languages.

does not see how it could ever be chosen as a symbolic representation of certain psychic unities. In a word, if we are to establish consciously and clearly a symbolic relation between sliminess and the sticky baseness of certain individuals, we must apprehend baseness already in sliminess and sliminess in certain baseness. Consequently the explanation by projection explains nothing since it takes for granted what it ought to explain. Furthermore even if it escaped this objection on principle, it would have to face another, drawn from experience and no less serious; the explanation by projection implies actually that the projecting subject has arrived by experience and analysis at a certain knowledge of the structure and effects of the attitudes which he calls slimy. According to this concept the recourse to sliminess does not as *knowledge* enrich our experience of human baseness. At the very most it serves as a thematic unity, as a picturesque rubric for bits of knowledge already acquired. On the other hand, sliminess proper, considered in its isolated state, will appear to us harmful in practice (because slimy substances stick to the hands, and clothes, and because they stain), but sliminess then is not *repugnant*. In fact the disgust which it inspires can be explained only by the combination of this physical quality with certain moral qualities. There would

have to be a kind of apprenticeship for learning the symbolic value of "slimy." But observation teaches us that even very young children show evidence of repulsion in the presence of something slimy, as if it were already
combined with the psychic. We know also
that from the time they know how to talk,
they *understand* the value of the words "soft,"
"low," *etc.,* when applied to the description
of feelings. All this comes to pass as if we
come to life in a universe where feelings and
acts are all charged with something material,
have a substantial stuff, are *really* soft, dull,
slimy, low, elevated, *etc.* and in which material substances have originally a psychic
meaning which renders them repugnant, hor-
rifying, alluring, *etc.* No explanation by projection or by analogy is acceptable here. To
sum up, it is impossible to derive the value of
the psychic symbolism of "slimy" from the
brute quality of the "this" and equally impossible to project the meaning on the *this*
in terms of a *knowledge* of psychic attitudes.
How then are we to conceive of this immense
and universal symbolism which is translated
by our repulsion, our hates, our sympathies,
our attractions toward objects whose materiality must on principle remain non-meaning-
ful? To progress in this study it is necessary to
abandon a certain number of postulates. In
particular we must no longer postulate *a pri-*

ori that the attribution of sliminess to a particular feeling is only an image and not knowledge. We must also refuse to admit—until getting fuller information—that the psychic allows us to form the physical matter symbolically or that our experience with human baseness has any priority over the apprehension of the "slimy" as meaningful.

Let us return to the original project. It is a project of appropriation. It compels the *slimy* to reveal its being; since the upsurge of the for-itself into being is appropriative, the slimy when perceived is "a slimy to be possessed"; that is, the original bond between the slimy and myself is that I form the project of being the foundation of its being, inasmuch as it is myself ideally. From the start then it appears as a possible "myself" to be established; from the start it has a psychic quality. That definitely does not mean that I endow it with a soul in the manner of primitive animism, nor with metaphysical virtues, but simply that even its materiality is revealed to me as having a psychic meaning—this psychic meaning, furthermore, is identical with the symbolic value which the slimy has in relation to being-in-itself. This appropriative mode of forcing the slimy to produce all its meanings can be considered as a formal *a priori*, although it is a free project and although it identifies itself with the being of the for-itself. In fact the appropriative mode does not depend originally on the mode of being of the slimy but only on its brute being there, on its pure encountered existence; it is like any other encounter since it is a simple project of appropriation, since it is not distinguished in any way from the pure "there is" and since it is, according to whether we consider it from one point of view or the other, either pure freedom or pure nothingness. But it is precisely within the limits of this appropriative project that the slimy reveals itself and develops its sliminess. From the first appearance of the slimy, this sliminess is already a response to a demand, already a *bestowal of self;* the slimy appears as already the plan for a fusion of the world with myself. What it teaches me about the world, that it is like a *leech sucking me,* is already a reply to a concrete question; it responds with its very being, with its mode of being, with all its matter. The response which it gives is at the same time fully appropriate to the question and yet opaque and indecipherable, for it is rich with all its inexpressible materiality. It is clear inasmuch as the reply is exactly appropriate; the slimy lets itself be apprehended as that which I lack; it lets itself be examined by an appropriative inquiry; it allows its sliminess to be revealed to this appropriative inquiry. Yet it is opaque because if the meaningful form is evoked in the slimy by the for-itself, all its sliminess comes to succour and replenish it. We are referred then to a meaning which is full and dense, and this meaning releases for us first being-in-itself in so far as the slimy is at the moment that which is manifesting the world, and second an outline of ourselves, in so far as the appropriation outlines something as an act dissolving itself into the slimy.

What comes back to us then as an objective quality is a new *nature* which is neither material (and physical) nor psychic, but which transcends the opposition of the psychic and the physical, by discovering itself to us as the ontological expression of the entire world; that is, which offers itself as a rubric for classifying all the "thises" in the world, so that we have to deal with material organizations or transcended transcendences. This means that the apprehension of the slimy as such has, by the same stroke, created for the in-itself of the world a particular mode of giving itself. In its own way it symbolizes being; that is, so long as the contact with the slimy endures, everything takes place for us as if sliminess were the meaning of the entire world or the unique mode of being of being-it-itself—in the same way as for the primitive class of lizards all objects *are* lizards.

What mode of being is symbolized by the slimy? I see first that it is the homogeneity and the imitation of liquidity. A slimy substance like pitch is an aberrant fluid. At first, with the appearance of a fluid it manifests to us a being which is everywhere fleeing and yet everywhere similar to itself, which on all sides escapes yet on which one can float, a being without danger and without memory, which eternally is changed into itself, on which one leaves no mark and which could not leave a mark on us, a being which slides and on which one can slide, which can be possessed by something sliding (by a rowboat, a motor boat, or water ski), and which never possesses because it rolls over us, a being which is eternity and infinite temporality because it is a perpetual change without anything which changes, a being which best symbolizes in this synthesis of eternity and temporality, a possible fusion of the for-itself as pure temporality and the in-itself as pure eternity. But immediately the slimy reveals itself as essentially ambiguous because its fluidity exists in slow motion; there is a sticky thickness in its liquidity; it represents in itself a dawning triumph of the solid over the liquid—that is, a tendency of the indifferent in-itself which represents pure solid, to fix the liquidity, to absorb the for-itself which ought to dissolve it.

Slime is the agony of water. It presents itself as a phenomenon in process of becoming; it does not have the permanence within change that water has but on the contrary represents an accomplished break in a change of states. This fixed instability in the slimy discourages possession. Water is more fleeting, but it can be possessed in its very flight as something fleeing. The slimy flees with a heavy flight which has the same relation to water as the unwieldy earthbound flight of the chicken has to that of the hawk. Even this flight can not be possessed because it denies itself as flight. It is already almost a solid permanence. Nothing testifies more clearly to its ambiguous character as a "substance in between two states" than the slowness with which the slimy melts into itself. A drop of water touching the surface of a large body of water is instantly transformed into the body of water; we do not see the operation as buccal absorption, so to speak, of the drop of water by the body of water but rather as a spiritualizing and breaking down of the individuality of a single being which is dissolved in the great All from which it had issued. The symbol of the body of water seems to play a very important role in the construc-

tion of pantheistic systems; it reveals a particular type of relation between beings. But
if we consider the slimy,[6] we note that it presents a constant hysteresis in the phenomenon
of being transmuted into itself. The honey
which slides off my spoon on to the honey contained in the jar first sculptures the surface
by fastening itself on it in relief, and its fusion
with the whole is presented as a gradual sink-
ing, a collapse which appears at once as a *de-
flation* (think for example of children's pleasure in playing with a toy which whistles when
inflated and groans mournfully when deflat-
ing[7]) and as a *display*—like the flattening out
of the full breasts of a woman who is lying on
her back. In the slimy substance which dis-
solves into itself there is a visible resistance,
like the refusal of an individual who does not
want to be annihilated in the whole of being,
and at the same time a softness pushed to
its ultimate limit. For the *soft* is only an annihilation which is stopped half way, the soft
is what furnishes us with the best image of
our own destructive power and its limitations. The slowness of the disappearance of
the slimy drop in the bosom of the whole is

[6] Although slime has mysteriously preserved *all* fluidity
in slow motion, it must not be confused with purées where
fluidity roughly outlined, undergoes abrupt breaks and
blocks and where the substance after a preliminary plan
of pouring, rolls abruptly head over heels.

[7] In the original the reference is to gold-beater's skin, a
thin membrane used in making gold leaf. Tr.

grasped first in *softness,* which is like a re-
tarded annihilation and seems to be playing
for time, but this softness lasts up to the end;
the drop is sucked into the body of the slimy
substance. This phenomenon gives rise to
several characteristics of the slimy. First it is
soft to touch. Throw water on the ground;
it *runs.* Throw a slimy substance; it draws
itself out, it displays itself, it flattens itself out,
it is *soft;* touch the slimy; it does not flee, it
yields. There is in the very fact that we cannot grasp water a pitiless hardness which
gives to it a secret sense of being *metal;*
finally it is incompressible like steel. The
slimy is compressible. It gives us at first the
impression that it is a being which can be *possessed.* Doubly so: its sliminess, its adherence
to itself prevent it from escaping; I can take it
in my hands, separate a certain quantity of
honey or of pitch from the rest in the jar, and
thereby create an individual object by a continuous creation; but at the same time the
softness of this substance which is squashed in
my hands gives me the impression that I am
perpetually *destroying* it.

Actually we have here the image of destruc-
tion-creation. The slimy is *docile.* Only at the
very moment when I believe that I possess it,
behold by a curious reversal, *it* possesses me.
Here appears its essential character: its soft-

ness is leech-like. If an object which I hold in my hands is solid, I can let go when I please; its inertia symbolizes for me my total power; I give it its foundation, but it does not furnish any foundation for me; the For-itself collects the In-itself in the object and raises the object to the dignity of the In-itself without compromising itself (i.e., the self of the For-itself) but always remaining an assimilating and creative power; It is the For-itself which absorbs the In-itself. In other words, possession asserts the primacy of the For-itself in the synthetic being "In-itself-For-itself." Yet here is the slimy reversing the terms; the For-itself is suddenly *compromised.* I open my hands, I want to let go of the slimy and it sticks to me, it draws me, it sucks at me. Its mode of being is neither the reassuring inertia of the solid nor the dynamism like that in water which is exhausted in fleeing from me. It is a soft, yielding action, a moist and feminine sucking, it lives obscurely under my fingers, and I sense it like a dizziness; it draws me to it as the bottom of a precipice might draw me. There is something like a tactile fascination in the slimy. I am no longer the master in *arresting* the process of appropriation. It continues. In one sense it is like the supreme docility of the possessed, the fidelity of a dog who *gives himself* even when one does not

want him any longer and in another sense
there is underneath this docility the sly appropriation of the possessed.

Here we can see the symbol which abruptly
discloses itself: there exists a poisonous possession; there is a possibility that the In-itself
might absorb the For-itself; that is, that a
being might be constituted in a manner just
the reverse of the "In-itself-For-itself," and
that in this new being the In-itself would
draw the For-itself into its contingency, into
its indifferent externality, into its foundationless existence. At this instant I suddenly
understand the snare of the slimy: it is a
fluidity which holds me and which compro-
mises me; I can not *slide* on this slime, all its
suction cups hold me back; it can not slide
over me; it clings to me like a leech. The sliding however is not simply denied as in the
case of the solid; it is *degraded*. The slimy
seems to lend itself to me, it invites me, for a
body of slime at rest is not noticeably distinct
from a body of very dense liquid. But it is a
trap. The sliding is *sucked* in by the sliding
substance, and it leaves its traces upon me.
The slime is like a liquid seen in a nightmare,
where all its properties are animated by a
sort of life and turn back against me. Slime is
the revenge of the In-itself. A sickly-sweet,
feminine revenge which may be symbolized
on another level by the quality sugary. This is

why the sugarylike sweetness to the taste—
an indelible sweetness, which remains indefinitely in the mouth even after swallowing
—perfectly completes the essence of the slimy.
A sugary sliminess is the ideal of the slimy; it
symbolizes the sugary death of the For-itself
(like that of the wasp which sinks into the
jam and drowns in it) .

But at the same time the slimy is *myself,*
from the very fact that I plan an appropriation of the slimy substance. That sucking of
the slimy which I feel on my hands outlines a
kind of continuity of the slimy substance in
myself. These long, soft strings of substance
which fall from me to the slimy body (when,
for example, I plunge my hand into it and
then pull it out again) symbolize a rolling off
of myself in the slime. And the hysteresis
which I establish in the fusion of the ends of
these strings with the larger body, symbolizes
the resistance of my being to absorption into
the In-itself. If I dive into the water, if I
plunge into it, if I let myself sink in it, I experience no discomfort, for I do not have any
fear whatsoever that I may dissolve in it; I
remain a solid in its liquidity. If I sink in the
slimy, I feel that I am going to be lost in it;
that is, that I may dissolve in the slime precisely because the slimy is in process of solidification. The sticky would present the
same aspect as the slimy from this point of

view, but it does not have the same fascination, it does not compromise because it is inert. In the very apprehension of the slimy there is a gluey substance, compromising and without equilibrium like the haunting memory of a *metamorphosis*.

To touch the slimy is to risk being dissolved into slime. Now this dissolution by itself is frightening enough, because it is the absorption of the For-itself by the In-itself as ink is absorbed by a blotter. But it is still more frightening in that the metamorphosis is not just into a thing (bad as that would be) but into slime. Even if I could conceive of a liquefaction of myself; that is, a transformation of my being into water, I would not be inordinately affected because water is the symbol of consciousness—its movement, its fluidity, its deceptive appearance of being solid, its perpetual flight—everything in it recalls the For-itself; to such a degree that psychologists who first noted the characteristic of *duration* of consciousness (James, Bergson) have very often compared it to a river. A river best evokes the image of the constant interpenetration of the parts by a whole and their perpetual dissociation and free movement.

But the slimy offers a horrible image; it is horrible in itself for a consciousness to *become slimy*. This is because the being of the

slimy is a soft clinging, there is a sly solidarity
and complicity of all its leechlike parts, a
vague, soft effort made by each to individualize itself, followed by a falling back and
flattening out that is emptied of the individual, sucked in on all sides by the substance. A consciousness which became slimy
would be transformed by the thick stickiness
of its ideas. From the time of our rise into the
world, we are haunted by the image of a consciousness which would like to launch forth
into the future, toward a projection of self,
and which in the very moment when it was
conscious of arriving there would be slyly
held back by the invisible suction of the past
and which would have to assist in its own slow
dissolution in this past which it was fleeing,
would have to aid in the invasion of its project by a thousand parasites until finally it
completely lost itself. The "flight of ideas"
which influences psychoses gives us the best
image of this horrible condition. But what is
it then which expresses this fear on the ontological plane if not exactly the flight of the
For-itself before the In-itself of facticity; that
is, exactly temporalization. The horror of the
slimy is the horrible fear that time might become slimy, that facticity might progress continually and insensibly and absorb the For-
itself which *makes it exist*. It is the fear not
of death, not of the pure In-itself, not of noth-

ingness, but of a particular type of being, which does not actually exist any more than the In-itself-For-itself and which is only *represented* by the slimy. It is an ideal being which I reject with all my strength and which haunts me as *value* haunts my being, an ideal being in which the foundationless In-itself has priority over the For-itself. We shall call it an *Antivalue*.

Thus in the project of appropriating the slimy, the sliminess is revealed suddenly as a symbol of an antivalue; it is a type of being not realized but threatening which will perpetually haunt consciousness as the constant danger which it is fleeing, and hence it will suddenly transform the project of appropriation into a project of flight. Something has appeared which is not the result of any prior experience but only of the preontological comprehension of the In-itself and the For-itself, and this is the peculiar meaning of the slimy. In one sense it is an experience since sliminess is an intuitive discovery; in another sense it is like the discovery of a venture of being. Henceforth for the For-itself there appears a new danger, a threatening mode of being which must be avoided, a concrete category which it will discover everywhere. The slimy does not symbolize any psychic attitude *a priori;* it manifests a certain relation of being with itself and this relation has originally a psychic quality because I have discovered it in a plan of appropriation and because the sliminess has returned my image to me. Thus I am enriched from my first contact with the slimy, by a valid ontological pattern beyond the distinction between psychic and non-psychic, which will interpret the meaning of being and of all the existents of a certain category, this category arising, moreover, like an empty framework *before* the experience with different kinds of sliminess. I have projected it into the world by my original project when faced with the slimy; it is an objective structure of the world and at the same time an anti-value; that is, it determines an area where slimy objects will arrange themselves. Henceforth each time that an object will manifest to me this relation of being, whether it is a matter of a handshake, of a smile, or of a thought, it will be apprehended by definition as slimy; that is, beyond its phenomenal context, it will appear to me as constituting along with pitch, glue, honey, *etc.* the great ontological region of sliminess.

Conversely, to the extent that the *this* which I wish to appropriate, represents the entire world, the slimy, from my first intuitive contact, appears to me rich with a host of obscure meanings and references which surpass it. The slimy is discovered in itself as "much more than the slimy." From the moment of its appearance it transcends all distinctions between psychic and physical, between the brute existent and the meanings of the world; it is a possible meaning of being. The first experience which the infant can have with the slimy enriches him psychologically and morally; he will not need to reach adulthood to discover the kind of sticky baseness which we indicate by the figure "slimy"; it is there near him in the very sliminess of honey or of glue. What we say concerning the slimy is valid for all the objects which surround the child. The simply revelation of their matter extends his horizon to the extreme limits of being and bestows upon him at the same stroke a collection of clues for deciphering the being of all human facts. This certainly does not mean that he *knows* from the start the "ugliness," the "characteristics," or the "beauties" of existence. He is merely in possession of all the *meanings of being* of which ugliness and beauty, attitudes, psychic traits, sexual relations, *etc.* will never be more than particular exemplifications. The gluey, the sticky, the hazy, *etc.* holes in the sand and in the earth, caves, the light, the night, *etc.*—all reveal to him modes of pre-psychic and presexual being which he will spend the rest of his life explaining. There is no such thing as an "innocent" child. We will gladly recognize along with the Freudians the innumerable relations existing between sexuality and certain matter and forms in the child's environment. But we do not understand by this that a sexual instinct already constituted has charged them with a sexual significance. On the contrary it seems to us that this matter and these forms are apprehended in themselves, and they reveal to the child modes of being and relations to the being of the For-itself which will illuminate and shape his sexuality.

To cite only one example—many psychoanalysts have been struck by the attraction which all kinds of holes exert on the child (whether holes in the sand or in the ground, crypts, caves, hollows, or whatever), and they have explained this attraction either by the anal character of infant sexuality, or by prenatal shock, or by a presentiment of the adult sexual act. But we can not accept any of these explanations. The idea of "birth trauma" is highly fantastic. The comparison of the hole to the feminine sexual organ supposes in the child an experience which he can not possibly have had or a presentiment which we can not justify. As for the child's anal sexuality, we would not think of denying it, but if it is going to illuminate the holes which he encounters in the perceptual field and charge them with symbolism, then it is necessary that the child apprehend his anus

as a hole; to put it more clearly, the child
would have to apprehend the essence of the
hole, of the orifice, as corresponding to the
sensation which he receives from his anus. But
we have demonstrated sufficiently the subjective character of "my relation with my body"
so that we can understand the impossibility of
saying that the child apprehends a particular
part of his body as an objective structure of
the universe. It is only to another person that
the anus appears as an orifice. The child himself can never have experienced it as such;
even the intimate care which the mother gives
the child could not reveal the anus in this aspect, since the anus as an erogenous zone, or a
zone of pain is not provided with tactile
nerve endings. On the contrary it is only
through another—through the words which
the mother uses to designate the child's body
—that he learns that his anus is a *hole*. It is
the objective nature of the hole perceived
in the world which is going to illuminate for
him the objective structure and the meaning
of the anal zone and which will give a transcendent meaning to the erogenous sensations
which hitherto he limited to merely "existing." In itself then the *hole* is the symbol of a
mode of being which existential psychoanalysis must elucidate. We can not make such a
study here. One can see at once, however, that
the hole is originally presented as a nothing-

ness "to be filled" with my own flesh; the child can not restrain himself from putting his finger or his whole arm into the hole. It presents itself to me as the empty image of myself. I have only to crawl into it in order to make myself exist in the world which awaits me. The ideal of the hole is then an excavation which can be carefully moulded about my flesh in such a manner that by squeezing myself into it and fitting myself tightly inside it, I shall contribute to making a fullness of being exist in the world. Thus to plug up a hole means originally to make a sacrifice of my body in order that the plenitude of being may exist; that is, to subject the passion of the For-itself so as to shape, to perfect, and to preserve the totality of the In-itself.[8]

Here at its origin we grasp one of the most fundamental tendencies of human reality— the tendency to fill. We shall meet with this tendency again in the adolescent and in the adult. A good part of our life is passed in plugging up holes, in filling empty places, in realizing and symbolically establishing a plenitude. The child recognizes as the result of his first experiences that he himself has holes. When he puts his fingers in his mouth, he tries to wall up the holes in his face; he expects that his finger will merge with his lips

---

[8] We should note as well the importance of the opposite tendency, to poke through holes, which in itself demands an existential analysis.

and the roof of his mouth and block up the buccal orifice as one fills the crack in a wall with cement; he seeks again the density, the uniform and spherical plenitude of Parmenidean being; if he sucks his thumb, it is precisely in order to dissolve it, to transform it into a sticky paste which will seal the hole of his mouth. This tendency is certainly one of the most fundamental among those which serve as the basis for the act of eating; nourishment is the "cement" which will seal the mouth; to eat is among other things to be filled up.

It is only in those terms that we can pass on to sexuality. The obscenity of the feminine sex is that of everything which "gapes open." It is a *summons to being* as all holes are. In herself woman appeals to a strange flesh which is to transform her into a fullness of being by penetration and dissolution. Conversely woman senses her condition as an appeal precisely because she is "in the form of a hole." This is the true origin of Adler's complex. Beyond any doubt her sex is a mouth and a voracious mouth which devours the penis—a fact which can easily lead to the idea of castration. The amorous act is the castration of the man; but this is above all because sex is a hole. We have to deal with a *presexual* contribution which will become one of the components of sexuality as an empirical, complex, human attitude but which far from deriving its origin from the sexed being has nothing in common with basic sexuality, the nature of which we have explained in Book III. Nevertheless the experience with the hole, when the infant sees reality, envelops the ontological presentiment of sexual experience in general; it is with his flesh that the child stops up the hole, and the hole before all sexual specification, is an obscene expectation, an appeal to the flesh.

We can see the importance which the elucidation of these immediate and concrete existential categories will assume for existential psychoanalysis. In this way we can apprehend the very general projects of human reality. But what chiefly interests the psychoanalyst is to determine the free project of the unique person in terms of the individual relation which unites him to these various symbols of being. I can love slimy contacts, have a horror of holes, *etc.* That does not mean that for me the slimy, the greasy, a hole, *etc.* have lost their general ontological meaning, but on the contrary that *because* of this meaning, I determine myself in this or that manner in relation to them. If the slimy is indeed the symbol of a being in which the for-itself is swallowed up by the in-itself, what kind of a person am I if in encountering others, I love the slimy? To what fundamental project of myself am I referred if I want to explain this love of an ambiguous, sucking in-itself? In this way *tastes* do not remain irreducible data; if one knows how to question them, they reveal to us the fundamental projects of the person. Down to even our alimentary preferences they all have a meaning. We can account for this fact if we will reflect that each taste is presented, not as an absurd *datum* which we must excuse but as an evident value. If I like the taste of garlic, it seems irrational to me that other people can not like it.

To eat is to appropriate by destruction; it is at the same time to be filled up with a certain being. And this being is given as a synthesis of temperature, density, and flavor proper. In a word this synthesis signifies *a certain being;* and when we eat, we do not limit ourselves to *knowing* certain qualities of this being through taste; by tasting them we appropriate them. Taste is assimilation; by the very act of biting the tooth reveals the density of a body which it is transforming into gastric contents. Thus the synthetic intuition of food is in itself an assimilative destruction. It reveals to me the being which I am going to make my flesh. Henceforth, what I accept or what I reject with disgust is the very being of that existent, or if you prefer, the totality of the food proposes to me a certain mode of being of the being which I accept or refuse. This totality is organized as a form in which less intense qualities of density and of temperature are effaced behind the flavor proper which *expresses* them. The *sugary,* for example, *expresses* the slimy when we eat a spoonful of honey or molasses, just as an analytical function expresses a geometric curve. This means that all qualities which are not strictly speaking flavor but which are massed, melted, buried in the flavor, represent the *matter* of the flavor. (The piece of chocolate which at first offers a resistance to my tooth, soon abruptly gives way and crumbles; its resistance first, then its crumbling *is* chocolate.) In addition they are united to certain temporal characteristics of flavor; that is, to its mode of temporalization. Certain tastes give themselves all at once, some are like delayed-action fuses, some give themselves up by growing faint, certain ones dwindle slowly until they disappear, and still others vanish at the very moment of possession. These qualities are organized along with density and temperature; in addition on another level they express the visual aspect of the nutriment. If I eat a rose cake; the taste of it is rose; the light sugary perfume, the oiliness of the butter cream *are* the rose. Thus I eat the rose as I see the sugary. We conclude that flavor, due to this fact, has a complex architecture and differentiated matter; it is this structured matter—which represents for us a particular type of being—that we can assimilate or reject with nausea, according to our original project. It is not a matter of indifference whether we like oysters or clams, snails or shrimp, if we are ever to know how to unravel the existential significance of these foods.

Generally speaking there is no irreducible taste or inclination. They all represent a certain appropriative choice of being. It is up to existential psychoanalysis to compare and classify them. Ontology abandons us here; it has merely enabled us to determine the ultimate ends of human reality, its fundamental possibilities and the value which haunts it. Each human reality is at the same time a direct project to metamorphose its own For-itself into an In-itself-For-itself and a project of the appropriation of the world as a totality of being-in-itself, in the form of a fundamental quality. Every human reality is a passion in that it projects losing itself so as to establish being and by the same stroke to constitute the In-itself which escapes contingency by being its own foundation, the *Ens causa sui,* which religions call God. Thus the passion of man is the reverse of that of Christ, for man loses himself as man in order that God may be born. But the idea of God is contradictory and we lose ourselves in vain. Man is a useless passion.

I

BAD FAITH AND FALSEHOOD

THE HUMAN being is not only the being by whom négatités[1] are disclosed in the world; he is also the one who can take negative attitudes with respect to himself. In our Introduction we defined consciousness as "a being, the nature of which is to question its own being, that being implying a being other than itself." But now that we have examined the meaning of "the question," we can at present also write the formula thus: "Consciousness is a being, the nature of which is to be conscious of the nothingness of its being." In a prohibition or a veto, for example, the human being denies a future transcendence. But this negation is not verifiable. My consciousness is not restricted to considering a négatité. It constitutes itself in its own substance as the annihilation of a possibility which another hu-

---

[1] *Négatités*: Sartre's word for kinds of human experience which blend negative and positive—such as absence, change, otherness, repulsion, regret, *etc.* Discussed in Part Two.

man reality projects as its possibility. For that reason it must arise in the world as a *Not;* it is as a Not that the slave first apprehends the master, or that the prisoner who is trying to escape sees the guard who is watching him. There are even men (e.g., caretakers, overseers, gaolers,) whose social reality is uniquely that of the Not, who will live and die, having forever been only a Not upon the earth. Others so as to make the Not a part of their very subjectivity, establish their human personality as a perpetual negation. This is the meaning and function of what Scheler calls "the man of resentment"—in reality, the Not. But there exist more subtle behaviours, the description of which will lead us further into the inwardness of consciousness. Irony is one of these. In irony a man annihilates what he posits within one and the same act; he leads us to believe in order not to be believed; he affirms to deny and denies to affirm; he creates a positive object but it has no being other than its nothingness. Thus attitudes of negation toward the self permit us to raise a new question: What are we to say is the nature of man who has the possibility of denying himself? But it is out of the question to discuss the attitude of "self-negation" in its universality. The kinds of behaviour which can be ranked under this heading are too diverse; we risk retaining only the abstract form

of them. It is best to choose and to examine
one determined attitude which is essential to
human reality and which is such that consciousness instead of directing its negation
outward turns it toward itself. This attitude, it seems to me, is *bad faith* (*mauvaise
foi*).

Frequently this is identified with falsehood. We say indifferently of a person that
he shows signs of bad faith or that he lies to
himself. We shall willingly grant that bad
faith is a lie to oneself, on condition that we
distinguish the lie to oneself from lying in
general. Lying is a negative attitude, we will
agree to that. But this negation does not bear
on consciousness itself; it aims only at the
transcendent. The essence of the lie implies
in fact that the liar actually is in complete
possession of the truth which he is hiding. A
man does not lie about what he is ignorant
of; he does not lie when he spreads an error of
which he himself is the dupe; he does not lie
when he is mistaken. The ideal description
of the liar would be a cynical consciousness,
affirming truth within himself, denying it in
his words, and denying that negation as such.
Now this doubly negative attitude rests on
the transcendent; the fact expressed is transcendent since it does not exist, and the original negation rests on a *truth;* that is, on a
particular type of transcendence. As for the

inner negation which I effect correlatively
with the affirmation for myself of the truth,
this rests on *words;* that is, on an event in the
world. Furthermore the inner disposition of
the liar is positive; it could be the object of an
affirmative judgment. The liar intends to deceive and he does not seek to hide this intention from himself nor to disguise the translucency of consciousness; on the contrary, he
has recourse to it when there is a question of
deciding secondary behaviour. It explicitly
exercises a regulatory control over all attitudes. As for his flaunted intention of telling
the truth ("I'd never want to deceive you!
This is true! I swear it!")—all this, of course,
is the object of an inner negation, but also it
is not recognized by the liar as *his* intention.
It is played, imitated, it is the intention of the
character which he plays in the eyes of his
questioner, but this character, precisely because he *does not exist,* is a transcendent.
Thus the lie does not put into play the inner
structure of present consciousness; all the ne-
gations which constitute it bear on objects
which by this fact are removed from consciousness. The lie then does not require special ontological foundation, and the explanations which the existence of negation in general requires are valid without change in the
case of deceit. Of course we have described the
ideal lie; doubtless it happens often enough

that the liar is more or less the victim of his
lie, that he half persuades himself of it. But
these common, popular forms of the lie are
also degenerate aspects of it; they represent
intermediaries between falsehood and bad
faith. The lie is a behaviour of transcendence.

The lie is also a normal phenomenon of
what Heidegger calls the *"Mit-sein."* [2] It presupposes my existence, the existence of the
other, my existence *for* the other, and the
existence of the other *for* me. Thus there is
no difficulty in holding that the liar must
make the project of the lie in entire clarity
and that he must possess a complete comprehension of the lie and of the truth which he
is altering. It is sufficient that an opaqueness
of principle hide his intentions from *the
other,* it is sufficient that the other can take
the lie for truth. By the lie consciousness affirms that it exists by nature as *hidden from
the other;* it utilizes for its own profit the ontological duality of myself and myself in the
eyes of others.

The situation can not be the same for bad
faith if this, as we have said, is indeed a lie
to oneself. To be sure, the one who practices
bad faith is hiding a displeasing truth or presenting as truth a pleasing untruth. Bad faith
then has in appearance the structure of falsehood. Only what changes everything is the

[2] A "being-with" others in the world. Tr.

fact that in bad faith it is from myself that I
am hiding the truth. Thus the duality of the
deceiver and the deceived does not exist here.
Bad faith on the contrary implies in essence
the unity of *a single* consciousness. This does
not mean that it can not be conditioned by
the *"Mit-sein"* like all other phenomena of
human reality, but the *"Mit-sein"* can call
forth bad faith only by presenting itself as a
situation which bad faith permits surpassing; bad faith does not come from outside to
human reality. One does not undergo his bad
faith; one is not infected with it; it is not a
state. But consciousness affects itself with bad
faith. There must be an original intention
and a project of bad faith; this project implies a comprehension of bad faith as such
and a pre-reflective apprehension (of) consciousness[3] as affecting itself with bad faith. It
follows first that the one to whom the lie is
told and the one who lies are one and the
same person, which means that I must know
in my capacity as deceiver the truth which is
hidden from me in my capacity as the one deceived. Better yet I must know the truth
very exactly in *order* to conceal it more care-

[3] Sartre has explained earlier in *Being and Nothingness*
that he will put the *of* in parentheses in such expressions
as "consciousness of something" so as to show the lack of
any real separation between consciousness and that which
it is conscious of being. Consciousness is never, he reminds
us, the same as knowledge. Tr.

fully—and this not at two different moments, which at a pinch would allow us to reestablish a semblance of duality—but in the unitary structure of a single project. How then can the lie subsist if the duality which conditions it is suppressed?

To this difficulty is added another which is derived from the total translucency of consciousness. That which affects itself with bad faith must be conscious (of) its bad faith since the being of consciousness is consciousness of being. It appears then that I must be in good faith, at least to the extent that I am conscious of my bad faith. But then this whole psychic system is annihilated. We must agree in fact that if I deliberately and cynically attempt to lie to myself, I fail completely in this undertaking; the lie falls back and collapses under my regard; it is ruined *from behind* by the very consciousness of lying to myself which pitilessly constitutes itself well within my project as its very condition. We have here an *evanescent* phenomenon which exists only in and through its own differentiation. To be sure, these phenomena are frequent and we shall see that there is in fact an "evanescence" in bad faith. It is evident that it vacillates continually between good faith and cynicism: Even though the existence of bad faith is very precarious, and though it belongs to the

kind of psychic structures which we might
call "metastable," [4] it presents nonetheless
an autonomous and durable form. It can even
be the normal aspect of life for a very great
number of people. A person can *live* in bad
faith, which does not mean that he does not
have abrupt awakenings to cynicism or to
good faith, but which implies a constant and
particular style of life. Our embarrassment
then appears extreme since we can neither
reject nor comprehend bad faith.

To escape from these difficulties people
gladly have recourse to the unconscious. In
the psychoanalytical interpretaton, for example, they use the hypothesis of a censor,
conceived as a line of demarcation with cus-
toms, passport division, currency control, *etc.*
to reestablish the duality of the deceiver and
the deceived. Here instinct or, if you prefer,
original drives and complexes of drives constituted by our individual history, make up
reality. It is neither *true* nor *false* since it does
not exist *for itself.* It simply *is,* exactly like
this table, which is neither true nor false *in
itself* but simply *real.* As for the conscious
symbols of the instinct, this interpretation
takes them not for appearances but for real
psychic facts. Fear, forgetting, dreams exist
really by virtue of concrete facts of conscious-

[4] Sartre's own word, meaning subject to sudden changes
or transitions. Tr.

ness, in the same way as the words and the attitudes of the liar are concrete, really existing patterns of behaviour. The subject has the same relation to these phenomena as the deceived to the behaviour of the deceiver. He establishes them in their reality and must interpret them. There is a *truth* in the activities of the deceiver; if the deceived could reattach them to the situation where the deceiver establishes himself and to his project of the lie, they would become integral parts of truth, by virtue of the behaviour of lying. Similarly there is a truth in the symbolic arts; it is what the psychoanalyst discovers when he reattaches them to the historical situation of the patient, to the unconscious complexes which they express, to the blocking of the censor. Thus the subject deceives himself about the *meaning* of his conduct, he apprehends it in its concrete existence but not in its *truth,* for lack of being able to derive it from an original situation and from a psychic constitution which remain alien to him.

By the distinction between the "id" and the "ego," Freud has cut the psychic whole into two. I *am* the ego but I am not the *id.* I hold no privileged position in relation to my unconscious psyche. I *am* my own psychic phenomena, in so far as I establish them in their conscious reality. For example, I am the impulse to steal this or that book from this bookstall. I am an integral part of the impulse; I bring it to light and I determine myself hand in hand with it to commit the theft. But I *am* not those psychic facts, in so far as I receive them passively and am obliged to resort to hypotheses about their origin and their true meaning, just as the scholar makes conjectures about the nature and essence of an external phenomenon. This theft, for example, which I interpret as an immediate impulse determined by the rarity, the interest, or the price of the volume which I am going to steal—it is in truth a process derived from self-punishment which is attached more or less directly to an Oedipus complex. The impulse toward the theft contains a truth which can be reached only by more or less probable hypotheses. The criterion of this truth will be the number of conscious psychic facts which it explains; from a more pragmatic point of view it will be also the success of the psychiatric cure which it allows. Finally the discovery of this truth will necessitate the co-operation of the psychoanalyst, who appears as the *mediator* between my unconscious drives and my conscious life. *The other* appears as being able to effect the synthesis between the unconscious thesis and the conscious antithesis. I can know myself only through the mediation of the other, which means that I stand in relation to *my* "id," in the position of *the other*. If I have a little knowledge of psychoanalysis, I can, under circumstances particularly favorable, try to psychoanalyze myself. But this attempt can succeed only if I distrust every kind of intuition, only if I apply to my case *from without,* abstract schemes and rules already learned. As for the results, whether they are obtained by my efforts alone or with the cooperation of a technician, they will never have the certainty which intuition confers; they will possess simply the always increasing probability of scientific hypotheses. The hypothesis of the Oedipus complex, like the atomic theory, is nothing but an "experimental idea"; as Pierce said, it is not to be distinguished from the totality of experiences which it allows to be realized and the results which it enables us to foresee. Thus psychoanalysis substitutes for the notion of bad faith, the idea of a lie without a liar; it allows me to understand how it is possible for me to be lied to without lying to myself since it places me in the same relation to myself that the other has in respect to me; it replaces the duality of the deceiver and the deceived, the essential condition of the lie, by that of the "id" and the "ego." It introduces into my subjectivity the deepest intersubjective structure of the *Mit-sein.* Can this explanation satisfy us?

Considered more closely the psychoanalytic

theory is not as simple as it first appears. It is not accurate to hold that the "id" is presented as a thing in relation to the hypothesis of the psychoanalyst, for a thing is indifferent to the conjectures which we make concerning it, while the "id" on the contrary is sensitive to them when we approach the truth. Freud in fact reports resistance when at the end of the first period the doctor is approaching the truth. This resistance is objective behaviour apprehended from without: the patient shows defiance, refuses to speak, gives fantastic accounts of his dreams, sometimes even takes himself completely away from the psychoanalytic cure. It is a fair question to ask what part of himself can thus resist. It can not be the "Ego," envisaged as a psychic totality of the facts of consciousness; this could not suspect that the psychiatrist is approaching the end since its relation to the *meaning* of its own reactions is exactly like that of the psychiatrist himself. At the very most it is possible for the ego to appreciate objectively the degree of probability in the hypotheses set forth, as a witness of the psychoanalysis might be able to do, according to the number of subjective facts which they explain. Furthermore, this probability would appear to the ego to border on certainty, which he could not take offence at since most of the time it is he who by a *conscious* decision is in pursuit of the psychoanalytic therapy. Are we to say that the patient is disturbed by the daily revelations which the psychoanalyst makes to him and that he seeks to remove himself, at the same time pretending in his own eyes to wish to continue the cure? In this case it is no longer possible to resort to the unconscious to explain bad faith; it is there in full consciousness, with all its contradictions. But this is not the way that the psychoanalyst means to explain this resistance; for him it is secret and deep, it comes from afar; it has its roots in the very thing which the psychoanalyst is trying to make clear.

Furthermore it is equally impossible to explain the resistance as emanating from the complex which the psychoanalyst wishes to bring to light. The complex as such is rather the collaborator of the psychoanalyst since it aims at expressing itself in clear consciousness, since it plays tricks on the censor and seeks to elude it. The only level on which we can locate the refusal of the subject is that of the censor. It alone can comprehend the questions or the revelations of the psychoanalyst as approaching more or less near to the real drives which it strives to repress—it alone because it alone *knows* what it is repressing.

If we reject the language and the materialistic mythology of psychoanalysis, we perceive that the censor in order to apply its activity with discernment, must know what it is repressing. In fact if we abandon all the metaphors representing the repression as the impact of blind forces, we are compelled to admit that the censor must choose and in order to choose must be aware of so doing. How could it happen otherwise that the censor allows lawful sexual impulses to pass through, that it permits needs (hunger, thirst, sleep) to be expressed in clear consciousness? And how are we to explain that it can relax its surveillance, that it can even be *deceived* by the disguises of the instinct? But it is not sufficient that it discern the condemned drives; it must also apprehend them as *to be repressed*, which implies in it at the very least an awareness of its activity. In a word, how could the censor discern the impulses needing to be repressed without being conscious of discerning them? How can we conceive of a knowledge which is ignorant of itself? To know is to know that one knows, said Alain. Let us say rather: all knowing is consciousness of knowing. Thus the resistance of the patient implies on the level of the censor an awareness of the thing repressed as such, a comprehension of the end toward which the questions of the psychoanalyst are leading, and an act of synthetic connection by which it compares the *truth* of the repressed complex to the psychoanalytic hypothesis which aims at it. These various operations in their turn imply that the censor is conscious (of) itself. But what type of self-consciousness can the censor have? It must be the consciousness (of) being conscious of the drive to be repressed, but precisely *in order not to be conscious of it*. What does this mean if not that the censor is in bad faith?

Psychoanalysis has not gained anything for us since in order to overcome bad faith, it has established between the unconscious and consciousness an autonomous consciousness in bad faith. The effort to establish a veritable duality and even a trinity (*Es, Ich, Ueberich* expressing themselves through the censor) has resulted in a merely verbal terminology. The very essence of the reflexive idea of hiding something from oneself implies the unity of one and the same psychic mechanism and consequently a double activity in the heart of unity, tending on the one hand to maintain and locate the thing to be concealed and on the other hand to repress and disguise it. Each of the two aspects of this activity is complementary to the other; that is, it implies the other in its being. By separating consciousness from the unconscious by means of the censor, psychoanalysis has not succeeded in dissociating the two phases of the act, since the libido is a blind conatus toward conscious expression and since the conscious phenomenon is a passive, faked result. Psychoanalysis has merely localized this double activity of repulsion and attraction on the level of the censor. Furthermore the problem still remains of accounting for the unity of the total phenomenon (the repression of the drive which disguises itself and "passes" in symbolic form), to establish comprehensible connections among its different phases. How can the repressed drive "disguise itself" if it does not include (1) the consciousness of being repressed, (2) the consciousness of having been pushed back because it is what it is, (3) a project of disguise? No mechanistic theory of condensation or of transference can explain these modifications by which the drive itself is affected, for the description of the process of disguise implies a veiled appeal to finality. And similarly how are we to account for the pleasure or the anguish which accompanies the symbolic and conscious satisfaction of the drive if consciousness does not include —beyond the censor—an obscure comprehension of the end to be attained as simultaneously desired and forbidden. By rejecting the conscious unity of the psyche, Freud is obliged to imply everywhere a magic unity linking distant phenomena across obstacles, just as sympathetic magic unites the spellbound person and the wax image fashioned in his likeness. The unconscious drive (*Trieb*)

through magic is endowed with the character "repressed" or "condemned," which completely pervades it, colors it, and magically
provokes its symbolism. Similarly the conscious phenomenon is entirely colored by its
symbolic meaning, although it can not apprehend this meaning by itself in clear consciousness.

Aside from its inferiority in principle, the
explanation by magic does not avoid the co-
existence—on the level of the unconscious, on
that of the censor, and on that of consciousness—of two contradictory, complementary
structures which reciprocally imply and destroy each other. Proponents of the theory
have hypostasized and "reified" bad faith;
they have not escaped it. That is what has
inspired a Viennese psychiatrist, Steckel, to
depart from the psychoanalytical tradition
and to write in *La femme frigide*:[5] "Every
time that I have been able to carry my investigations far enough, I have established that
the crux of the psychosis was conscious." In
addition the cases which he reports in his
work bear witness to a pathological bad faith,
which the Freudian doctrine can not account
for. There is the question, for example, of
women whom a marital infidelity has made
frigid; that is, they succeed in hiding from
themselves not complexes deeply sunk in half

[5] N.R.F.

physiological darkness, but acts of conduct which are objectively discoverable, which they can not fail to record at the moment when they perform them. Frequently in fact the husband reveals to Steckel that his wife has given objective signs of pleasure, but the woman when questioned will fiercely deny them. Here we find a pattern of detachment. Admissions which Steckel was able to draw out inform us that these pathologically frigid women apply themselves to detaching themselves in advance from the pleasure which they dread; many for example at the time of the sexual act, turn their thoughts away toward their daily occupations, make up their household accounts. Will anyone speak of an unconscious here? Yet if the frigid woman thus detaches her consciousness from the pleasure which she experiences, it is by no means cynically and in full agreement with herself; it is *in order to prove to herself* that she is frigid. We have in fact to deal with a phenomenon of bad faith since the efforts taken in order not to be present to the experienced pleasure imply the recognition that the pleasure is experienced; they imply it *in order to deny it*. But we are no longer on the ground of psychoanalysis. Thus on the one hand the explanation by means of the unconscious, due to the fact that it breaks the psychic unity, can not account for the facts

which at first sight it appeared to explain.
And on the other hand, there exists an infinity of types of behaviour in bad faith which
explicitly reject this kind of explanation because their essence implies that they can appear only in the translucency of consciousness.
We find that the problem which we had attempted to resolve is still untouched.

II

PATTERNS OF BAD FAITH

IF WE WISH to get out of this difficulty, we should examine more closely the patterns of bad faith and attempt a description of them. This description will permit us perhaps to fix more exactly the conditions for the possibility of bad faith; that is, to reply to the question we raised at the outset: "What must be the nature of man if he is to be capable of bad faith?"

Take the example of a woman who has consented to go out with a particular man for the first time. She knows very well the intentions which the man who is speaking to her cherishes regarding her. She knows also that it will be necessary sooner or later for her to make a decision. But she does not want to realize the urgency; she concerns herself only with what is respectful and discreet in the attitude of her companion. She does not apprehend this conduct as an attempt to achieve what we call "the first approach"; that is, she does not want to see the possibilities of temporal development which his conduct presents. She restricts this behaviour to what is in the present; she does not wish to read in the phrases which he addresses to her anything other than their explicit meaning. If he says to her, "I find you so attractive!" she disarms this phrase of its sexual background; she attaches to the conversation and to the behaviour of the speaker, the immediate meanings, which she imagines as objective qualities. The man who is speaking to her appears to her sincere and respectful as the table is round or square, as the wall coloring is blue or gray. The qualities thus attached to the person she is listening to are in this way fixed in a permanence like that of things, which is no other than the projection of the strict present of the qualities into the temporal flux. This is because she does not quite know what she wants, She is profoundly aware of the desire which she inspires, but the desire cruel and naked would humiliate and horrify her. Yet she would find no charm in a respect which would be only respect. In order to satisfy her, there must be a feeling which is addressed wholly to her *personality*—that is, to her full freedom— and which would be a recognition of her freedom. But at the same time this feeling must be wholly desire; that is, it must address itself to her body as object. This time then she refuses to apprehend the desire for what it is; she does not even give it a name; she recognizes it only to the extent that it transcends itself toward admiration, esteem, respect and that it is wholly absorbed in the more refined forms which it produces, to the extent of no longer figuring any more as a sort of warmth and density. But then suppose he takes her hand. This act of her companion risks changing the situation by calling for an immediate decision. To leave the hand there is to consent in herself to flirt, to engage herself. To withdraw it is to break the troubled and unstable harmony which gives the hour its charm. The aim is to postpone the moment of decision as long as possible. We know what happens next; the young woman leaves her hand there, but she *does not notice* that she is leaving it. She does not notice because it happens by chance that she is at this moment all intellect. She draws her companion up to the most lofty regions of sentimental speculation; she speaks of life, of her life, she shows herself in her essential aspect—a personality, a consciousness. And during this time the divorce of the body from the soul is accomplished; the hand rests inert between the warm hands of her companion—neither consenting nor resisting—a thing.

We shall say that this woman is in bad faith.

But we see immediately that she uses various procedures in order to maintain herself in this bad faith. She has disarmed the actions of her companion by reducing them to being only what they are; that is, to existing in the mode of the in-itself. But she permits herself to enjoy his desire, to the extent that she will apprehend it as not being what it is, will recognize its transcendence. Finally while sensing profoundly the presence of her own body—to the degree of being disturbed perhaps—she realizes herself as *not being* her own body and she contemplates it as though from above, as a passive object to which events can *happen,* but which can neither provoke them nor avoid them because all its possibilities are outside of it. What unity do we find in these various aspects of bad faith? It is a certain art of forming contradictory concepts which unite in themselves both an idea and the negation of that idea. The basic concept which is thus engendered, utilizes the double property of the human being, who is at once a *facticity* and a *transcendence.* These two aspects of human reality are in truth and ought to be capable of a valid coordination. But bad faith does not wish either to coordinate them nor to surmount them in a synthesis. Bad faith seeks to affirm their identity while preserving their differences. It must affirm facticity as *being* transcendence and

transcendence as *being* facticity, in such a way
that in the instant when a person apprehends
the one, he can find himself abruptly faced
with the other.

We can find the prototype of formulae
of bad faith in certain famous expressions
which have been rightly conceived to produce their whole effect in a spirit of bad faith.
Take for example the title of a work by Jac-
ques Chardonne, *Love Is Much More than
Love*.[1] We see here how unity is established
between *present* love in its facticity—"the
contact of two skins," sensuality, egoism,
Proust's mechanism of jealousy, Adler's battle
of the sexes, *etc.*—and love as transcendence
—Mauriac's "river of fire," the longing for
the infinite, Plato's *eros,* Lawrence's deep cos-
mic intuition, *etc.* Here we leave facticity to
find ourselves suddenly beyond the present
and the factual condition of man, beyond the
psychological, in the heart of metaphysics. On
the other hand, the title of a play by Sar-
ment, *I Am Too Great for Myself,*[2] which also
presents characters in bad faith, throws us
first into full transcendence in order suddenly
to imprison us within the narrow limits of
our factual essence. We will discover this
structure again in the famous phrase: "'He
has become what he was" or in its no less fa-

[1] *L'amour, c'est beaucoup plus que l'amour.*
[2] *Je suis trop grand pour moi.*

mous opposite: "Eternity at last changes each
man into himself." [3] It is well understood
that these various formulae have only the *appearance* of bad faith; they have been conceived in this paradoxical form explicitly to
shock the mind and discountenance it by an
enigma. But it is precisely this appearance
which is of concern to us. What counts here
is that the formulae do not constitute new,
solidly structured ideas, on the contrary, they
are formed so as to remain in perpetual disintegration and so that one may slide at any
time from naturalistic present to transcendence and *vice versa*. We can see the use which
bad faith can make of these judgments which
all aim at establishing that I am not what I
am. If I were not what I *am*, I could, for example, seriously consider an adverse criticism
which someone makes of me, question myself scrupulously, and perhaps be compelled
to recognize the truth in it. But thanks to
transcendence, I am not subject to all that I
am. I do not even have to discuss the justice
of the reproach. As Suzanne says to Figaro,
"To prove that I am right would be to recognize that I can be wrong." I am on a plane
where no reproach can touch me, since what
I really am is my transcendence. I flee from
myself, I escape myself, I leave my tattered

---

[3] *Il est devenu ce qu'il était.*
Tel qu'en lui-même enfin l'éternité le change.

garment in the hands of the fault-finder. But the ambiguity necessary for bad faith comes from the fact that I affirm here that I *am* my transcendence in the mode of being of a thing. It is only thus, in fact, that I can feel that I escape all reproaches. It is in the sense that our young woman purifies the desire of anything humiliating, by being willing to consider it only as pure transcendence, which she avoids even naming. But inversely "I am too great for myself" while showing our transcendence changed into facticity, is the source of an infinity of excuses for our failures or our weaknesses. Similarly the young coquette maintains transcendence to the extent that the respect, the esteem manifested by the actions of her admirer are already on the plane of the transcendent. But she arrests this transcendence, she glues it down with all the facticity of the present; respect is nothing other than respect, it is an arrested surpassing which no longer surpasses itself toward anything.

But although this *metastable* concept of "transcendence-facticity" is one of the most basic instruments of bad faith, it is not the only one of its kind. We can equally well use another kind of duplicity derived from human reality which we will express roughly by saying that its being-for-itself implies complementarily a being-for-others. Upon any one

of my activities it is always possible to con-
verge two regards, mine and that of another.
The activity will not present exactly the
same structure in each case. But as we shall
see later, as each regard perceives it, there is
not between these two aspects of my being,
any difference of appearance in being, as if
I were to my self the truth of myself and as if
the other possessed only a deformed image of
me. The equal dignity of being, possessed by
my being-for-another and by my being-for-
myself permits a perpetually disintegrating
synthesis and a perpetual game of evasion
from the for-itself to the for-others and from
the for-others to the for-itself. We have seen
also the use which our young lady made of
our being-in-the-midst-of-the-world; that is,
of our inert presence as a passive object
among other objects—in order to relieve herself suddenly from the functions of her being-in-the-world; that is, from the being
which causes there to exist a world by projecting itself beyond the world toward its own
possibilities. Let us note finally the confusing
syntheses which play on the annihilating ambiguity of these temporal ek-stases, affirming
at once that I am what I have been (the man
who deliberately *arrests himself* at one period in his life and refuses to take into consideration the later changes) and that I am
not what I have been (the man who in the

face of reproaches or rancour dissociates himself from his past by insisting on his freedom and on his perpetual re-creation). In all these concepts, which have only a transitive role in the reasoning and which are eliminated from the conclusion, like hypochondriacs in the calculations of physicians, we find again the same structure. We have to deal with human reality as a being which is what it is not and which is not what it is.

But what exactly is necessary in order for these concepts of disintegration to be able to receive even a pretence of existence, in order for them to be able to appear for an instant to consciousness, even in a process of evanescence? A quick examination of the idea of sincerity, the antithesis of bad faith, will be very instructive in this connection. Actually sincerity presents itself as a demand and consequently is not a *state*. Now what is the ideal to be attained in this case? It is necessary that a man be *for himself* only what he *is*. But is this not precisely the definition of the in-itself —or if you prefer—the principle of identity? To posit as an ideal the being of things, is this not to assert by the same stroke that this being does not belong to human reality and that the principle of identity, far from being a universal axiom universally applied, is only a synthetic principle enjoying a merely regional universality? Thus in order that the concepts of bad faith can put us under illusion at least for an instant, in order that the candour of "pure hearts" (*cf.* Gide, Kessel) can have validity for human reality as an ideal, the principle of identity must not represent a constitutive principle of human reality and human reality must not be necessarily what it is but must be able to be what it is not. What does this mean?

If man is what he is, bad faith is for ever impossible and candour ceases to be his ideal and becomes instead his being. But is man what he is? And more generally, how can he *be* what he is when he exists as consciousness of being? If candour or sincerity is a universal value, it is evident that the maxim "One must be what one is" does not serve uniquely as a regulating principle for judgements and concepts by which I express what I am. It posits not merely an ideal of knowing but an ideal of *being;* it proposes for us an absolute equivalence of being with itself as a prototype of being. In this sense it is necessary that we *make ourselves* what we are. But what *are we* then if we have the constant obligation to make ourselves what we are, if our mode of being is having the obligation to be what we are?

Let us consider this waiter in the café. His movement is quick and forward, a little too precise, a little too rapid. He comes toward the patrons with a step a little too quick. He bends forward a little too eagerly; his voice, his eyes express an interest a little too solicitous for the order of the customer. Finally there he returns, trying to imitate in his walk the inflexible stiffness of some kind of automaton while carrying his tray with the recklessness of a tight-rope-walker by putting it in a perpetually unstable, perpetually broken equilibrium which he perpetually reestablishes by a light movement of the arm and hand. All his behaviour seems to us a game. He applies himself to chaining his movements as if they were mechanisms, the one regulating the other, his gestures and even his voice seem to be mechanisms, he gives himself the quickness and pitiless rapidity of things. He is playing, he is amusing himself. But what is he playing? We need not watch long before we can explain it: he is playing *at being* a waiter in a café. There is nothing there to surprise us. The game is a kind of marking out and investigation. The child plays with his body in order to explore it, to take inventory of it; the waiter in the café plays with his condition in order to *realize* it. This obligation is not different from that which is imposed on all tradesmen. Their condition is wholly one of ceremony. The public demands of them that they realize it as a ceremony; there is the dance of the grocer,

of the tailor, of the auctioneer, by which they
endeavour to persuade their clientele that
they are nothing but a grocer, an auctioneer,
a tailor. A grocer who dreams is offensive to
the buyer, because such a grocer is not wholly
a grocer. Society demands that he limit himself to his function as a grocer, just as the soldier at attention makes himself into a soldier-
thing with a direct regard which does not see
at all, which is no longer meant to see, since
it is the rule and not the interest of the moment which determines the point he must
fix his eyes on (the sight "fixed at ten
paces"). There are indeed many precautions
to imprison a man in what he is, as if we lived
in perpetual fear that he might escape from
it, that he might break away and suddenly
elude his condition.

In a parallel situation, from within, the
waiter in the café can not be immediately a
café waiter in the sense that this inkwell *is* an
inkwell, or the glass is a glass. It is by no
means that he can not form reflective judgements or concepts concerning his condition.
He knows well what it "means": the obligation of getting up at five o'clock, of sweeping
the floor of the shop before the restaurant
opens, of starting the coffee pot going, *etc.* He
knows the rights which it allows: the right to
the tips, the right to belong to a union, *etc.*
But all these concepts, all these judgements

refer to the transcendent. It is a matter of abstract possibilities, of rights and duties conferred on a "person possessing rights." And it is precisely this person *who I have to be* (if I am the waiter in question) and who I am not. It is not that I do not wish to be this person or that I want this person to be different. But rather there is no common measure between his being and mine. It is a "representation" for others and for myself, which means that I can be he only in *representation*. But if I represent myself as him, I am not he; I am separated from him as the object from the subject, separated *by nothing,* but this nothing isolates me from him. I can not be he, I can only play *at being* him; that is, to imagine to myself that I am he. And thereby I affect him with nothingness. In vain do I fulfill the functions of a café waiter. I can be he only in the neutralized mode, as the actor is Hamlet, by mechanically making the *typical gestures* of my state and by aiming at myself as an imaginary café waiter through those gestures taken as an "analogue." [4] What I attempt to realize is a being-in-itself of the café waiter, as if it were not just in my power to confer their value and their urgency upon my duties and the rights of my position, as if it were not my free choice to get up each morn-

[4] *Cf. L'Imaginaire.* Conclusion.

ing at five o'clock or to remain in bed, even though it meant getting fired. As if from the very fact that I sustain this role in existence I did not transcend it on every side, as if I did not constitute myself as one *beyond* my condition. Yet there is no doubt that I *am* in a sense a café waiter—otherwise could I not just as well call myself a diplomat or a reporter? But if I am one, this can not be in the mode of being in-itself. I am a waiter in the mode *of being what I am not.*

Furthermore we are dealing with more than mere social conditions; I am never any one of my attitudes, any one of my actions. The good speaker is the one who *plays* at speaking, because he can not *be speaking.* The attentive pupil who wishes to *be* attentive, his eyes riveted on the teacher, his ears open wide, so exhausts himself in playing the attentive role that he ends up by no longer hearing anything. Perpetually absent to my body, to my acts, I am despite myself that "divine absence" of which Valéry speaks. I can not say either that I *am* here or that I *am* not here, in the sense that we say "that box of matches *is* on the table"; this would be to confuse my "being-in-the-world" with a "being-in-the-midst-of-the-world." Nor that I *am* standing, nor that I *am* seated; this would be to confuse my body with the idiosyncratic totality of which it is only one of the structures. On all sides I escape being and yet—I am.

But take a mode of being which concerns only myself: I am sad. One might think that surely I am the sadness in the mode of being what I am. What is the sadness, however, if not the intentional unity which comes to reassemble and animate the totality of my conduct? It is the meaning of this dull look with which I view the world, of my bowed shoulders, of my lowered head, of the listlessness in my whole body But at the very moment when I adopt each of these attitudes, do I not know that I shall not be able to hold on to it? Let a stranger suddenly appear and I will lift up my head, I will assume a lively cheerfulness. What will remain of my sadness except that I obligingly promise it an appointment for later after the departure of the visitor? Moreover is not this sadness itself a *conduct?* Is it not consciousness which affects itself with sadness as a magical recourse against a situation too urgent? [5] And in this case even, should we not say that being sad means firs' to make oneself sad? That may be, someone will say, but after all doesn't giving oneself the being of sadness mean to *receive* this being? It makes no difference from where I

[5] *Esquisse d'une théorie des émotions.* Hermann Paul. In English. *The Emotions. Outline of a Theory.* Philosophical Library. 1948.

receive it. The fact is that a consciousness
which affects itself with sadness *is* sad precisely for this reason. But it is difficult to comprehend the nature of consciousness; the being-sad is not a ready-made being which I
give myself as I can give this book to my
friend. I do not possess the property of *affecting myself with being*. If I make myself sad, I
must continue to make myself sad from beginning to end. I can not treat my sadness as
an impulse finally achieved and put it on file
without re-creating it, nor can I carry it in the
manner of an inert body which continues its
movement after the initial shock; there is no
inertia in consciousness. If I make myself sad,
it is because I *am* not sad—the being of the
sadness escapes me by and in the very act by
which I affect myself with it. The being-in-itself of sadness perpetually haunts my consciousness (of) being sad, but it is as a value
which I can not realize, it stands as a regula-
tive meaning of my sadness, not as its constitutive modality.

Someone may say that my consciousness at
least *is*, whatever may be the object or the
state of which it makes itself consciousness.
But how do we distinguish my consciousness
(of) being sad from sadness? Is it not all one?
It is true in a way that my consciousness *is*, if
one means by this that for another it is a part
of the totality of being on which judgements

can be brought to bear. But it should be noted, as Husserl clearly understood, that my consciousness appears originally to the other as an absence. It is the object always present as the *meaning* of all my attitudes and all my conduct—and always absent, for it gives itself to the intuition of another as a perpetual question, still better, as a perpetual freedom. When Pierre looks at me, I know of course that he is looking at me. His eyes, things in the world, are fixed on my body, a thing in the world—that is the objective fact of which I can say: it *is*. But it is also a fact *in the* world. The meaning of this look is not a fact in the world, and this is what makes me uncomfortable. Although I make smiles, promises, threats, nothing can get hold of the approbation, the free judgement which I seek; I know that it is always beyond. I sense it in my very attitude which is no longer like that of the worker toward the things he uses as instruments. My reactions, to the extent that I project myself toward the other, are no longer for myself but are rather mere *presentations;* they await being constituted as graceful or uncouth, sincere or insincere, *etc.* by an apprehension which is always beyond my efforts to provoke, an apprehension which will be provoked by my efforts only if of itself it lends them force, that is, only in so far as it causes itself to be provoked from without, *which is its own mediation with the transcendent.* Thus the objective fact of the being-in-itself of the consciousness of another is posited in order to disappear in negativity and in freedom: consciousness of another *is* as not being; its being-in-itself of "now" and of "here" is not to be.

To be conscious of another means to be conscious of what one is not.

Furthermore the being of my own consciousness does not appear to me as the consciousness of another. It exists because it makes itself, since its being is consciousness of being. But that means that making sustains being; consciousness has to be its own being, it is never sustained by being; it sustains being in the heart of subjectivity, which means once again that it is inhabited by being but that it is not being: *consciousness is not what it is.*

Under these conditions what can be the significance of the ideal of sincerity except an attempt impossible to achieve, of which the very meaning is in contradiction with the structure of my consciousness. To be sincere, we said, is to be what one is. That supposes that I am not originally what I am. But here naturally Kant's "You ought, therefore you can" is implicitly understood. I can *become* sincere; this is what my duty and my effort to achieve sincerity imply. But we definitely establish that the original structure of "not being what one is" renders impossible in advance all movement toward being in itself or "being what one is." And this impossibility is not hidden from consciousness; on the contrary, it is the very stuff of consciousness; it is the embarrassing constraint which we constantly experience; it is our very incapacity to recognize ourselves, to constitute ourselves as being what we are. It is this necessity which means that, as soon as we posit ourselves as a certain being by a legitimate judgement, based on inner experience or correctly deduced from *a priori* or empirical premises, by that very position we surpass this being—and that not toward another being but toward emptiness, toward *nothing*. How then can we blame another for not being sincere or rejoice in our own sincerity, since this sincerity appears to us at the same time to be impossible? How can we in conversation, in confession, in introspection, even attempt sincerity since the effort will by its very nature be doomed to failure and since at the very time when we announce it we have a prejudicative comprehension of its futility? In introspection I try to determine exactly what I am, to make up my mind to be my true self without delay—even though it means consequently to put myself searching for ways to change myself. But what does this mean if not

that I am constituting myself as a thing? Shall
I determine the ensemble of purposes and
motivations which have pushed me to do this
or that action? But this is already to postulate
a causal determinism which constitutes the
flow of my states of consciousness as a succession of physical states. Shall I uncover in
myself "drives," even though it be to affirm
them in shame? But is this not deliberately to
forget that these drives realize themselves
with my agreement, that they are not forces
of nature but that I lend them their efficacy
by a perpetually renewed decision concerning
their value. Shall I pass judgement on my
character, on my nature? Is this not to veil
from myself at that moment what I know only
too well, that I thus judge a past to which by
definition my present is not subject? The
proof of this is that the same man who in sincerity posits that he is what in actuality he
was, is indignant against the reproach of another and tries to disarm it by asserting that
he can no longer be what he was. We are readily astonished and upset when the penalties of
the court affect a man who in his new freedom
is no longer the guilty person he was. But at
the same time we require of this man that he
recognize himself as *being* this guilty one.
What then is sincerity except precisely a phenomenon of bad faith? Have we not shown
indeed that in bad faith human reality is con-

stituted as a being which is what it is not and which is not what it is?

Let us take an example: A homosexual frequently has an intolerable feeling of guilt and his whole existence is determined in relation to this feeling. One will readily foresee that he is in bad faith. In fact it frequently happens that this man, while recognizing his homosexual inclination, while avowing each and every particular misdeed which he has committed, refuses with all his strength to consider himself *"a pederast."* His case is always "different," peculiar; there enters into it something of a game, of chance, of bad luck; the mistakes are all in the past; they are explained by a certain conception of the beautiful which women can not satisfy; we should see in them the results of a restless search, rather than the manifestations of a deeply rooted tendency, *etc., etc.* Here is assuredly a man in bad faith who borders on the comic since, acknowledging all the facts which are imputed to him, he refuses to draw from them the conclusion which they impose. His friend who is his most severe critic, becomes irritated with this duplicity. The critic asks only one thing—and perhaps then he will show himself indulgent: that the guilty one recognize himself as guilty, that the homosexual declare frankly—whether humbly or boastfully matters little—*"I am a pederast."* We ask here:

Who is in bad faith? The homosexual or the champion of sincerity?

The homosexual recognizes his faults, but he struggles with all his strength against the crushing view that his mistakes constitute for him *a destiny*. He does not wish to let himself be considered as a thing. He has an obscure but strong feeling that an homosexual is not an homosexual as this table is a table or as this red-haired man is red-haired. It seems to him that he has escaped from each mistake as soon as he has posited it and recognized it; he even feels that the psychic duration by itself cleanses him from each misdeed, constitutes for him an undetermined future, causes him to be born anew. Is he wrong? Does he not recognize in himself the peculiar, irreducible character of human reality? His attitude includes then an undeniable comprehension of truth. But at the same time he needs this perpetual rebirth, this constant evasion in order to live; he must constantly put himself beyond reach in order to avoid the terrible judgement of collectivity. Thus he plays on the word *being*. He would be right actually if he understood the phrase, "I am not a pederast" in the sense of "I am not what I am." That is, if he declared to himself, "To the extent that a pattern of conduct is defined as the conduct of a pederast and to the extent that I have taken on this conduct, I am a pederast. But to the extent that human reality can not be finally defined by patterns of conduct, I am not one." But instead he slides surreptitiously towards a different connotation of the word "being." He understands "not being" in the sense of "not being in itself." He lays claim to "not being a pederast" in the sense in which this table *is not* an inkwell. He is in bad faith.

But the champion of sincerity is not ignorant of the transcendence of human reality and he knows how at need to appeal to it for his own advantage. He makes use of it even and brings it up in the present argument. Does he not wish, first in the name of sincerity, then of freedom, that the homosexual reflect on himself and acknowledge himself as an homosexual? Does he not let the other understand that such a confession will win indulgence for him? What does this mean if not that the man who will acknowledge himself as an homosexual will no longer be *the same* as the homosexual whom he acknowledges being, and that he will escape into the region of freedom and of good will. The critic asks the man then to be what he is in order no longer to be what he is. It is the profound meaning of the saying. "A sin confessed is half pardoned." He demands of the guilty one that he constitute himself as a thing, precisely in order no longer to treat him as a thing. And this contradiction is constitutive of the demand of sincerity. Who can not see how offensive to the other and how reassuring for me is a statement such as, "He's just a pederast," which removes a disturbing freedom from a trait and which aims at henceforth constituting all the acts of the other as consequences following strictly from his essence. That is actually what the critic is demanding of his victim— that he constitute himself as a thing, that he should entrust his freedom to his friend as a fief, in order that the friend should return it to him subsequently—like a suzerain to his vassal. The champion of sincerity is in bad faith to the degree that in order to reassure himself, he pretends to judge, to the extent that he demands that freedom as freedom constitute itself as a thing. We have here only one episode in that battle to the death of consciousnesses which Hegel calls "the relation of the master and the slave." A person appeals to another and demands that in the name of his nature as consciousness he should radically destroy himself as consciousness, but while making this appeal he leads the other to hope for a rebirth beyond this destruction.

Very well, someone will say, but our man is abusing sincerity, playing one side against the other. We should not look for sincerity in the relations of the *"Mit-sein"* but rather where it is pure—in the relations of a person with

himself. But who can not see that objective
sincerity is constituted in the same way? Who
can not see that the sincere man constitutes
himself as a thing in order to escape the condition of a thing by the same act of sincerity?
The man who confesses that he is evil has
exchanged his disturbing "freedom-for-evil"
for an inanimate character of evil; he *is* evil,
he clings to himself, he is what he is. But by
the same stroke, he escapes from that *thing*,
since it is he who contemplates it, since it depends on him to maintain it under his glance
or to let it collapse in an infinity of particular
acts. He derives a *merit* from his sincerity,
and the deserving man is not the evil man as
he is evil but as he is beyond his evilness. At
the same time the evil is disarmed since it is
nothing, save on the plane of determinism,
and since in confessing it, I posit my freedom
in respect to it; my future is virgin; everything is allowed to me. Thus the essential
structure of sincerity does not differ from that
of bad faith since the sincere man constitutes
himself as what he is *in order not to be it*. This
explains the truth recognized by all, that one
can fall into bad faith through being sincere.
As Valéry pointed out, this is the case with
Stendhal. Total, constant sincerity as a constant effort to adhere to oneself is by nature a
constant effort to dissociate oneself from oneself. A person frees himself from himself by

the very act by which he makes himself an object for himself. To draw up a perpetual inventory of what one is means constantly to redeny oneself and to take refuge in a sphere where one is no longer anything but a pure, free regard. The goal of bad faith, as we said, is to put oneself out of reach, it is an escape. Now we see that we must use the same terms to define sincerity. What does this mean?

In the final anlysis the goal of sincerity and the goal of bad faith are not so different. To be sure, there is a sincerity which bears on the past and which does not concern us here; I am sincere if I confess *having had* this pleasure or that intention. We shall see that if this sincerity is possible, it is because in his lapse in the past, the being of man is constituted as a being-in-itself. But here our concern is only with the sincerity which aims at itself in present immanence. What is its goal? To bring me to confess to myself what I am in order that I may finally coincide with my being; in a word, to cause myself to be in the mode of the in-itself, what I am in the mode of "not being what I am." Its assumption is that fundamentally I am already in the mode of the in-itself, what I have to be. Thus we find at the base of sincerity a continual game of mirror and reflection, a perpetual passage from the being which is what it is, to the being which is not what it is and inversely from the being which is not what it is to the being which is what it is. And what is the goal of bad faith? To cause me to be what I am, in the mode of "not being what one is," or not to be what I am in the mode of "being what one is." We find here the same playing with mirrors. In fact in order for me to have an intention of sincerity, I must at the outset simultaneously be and not be what I am. Sincerity does not assign to me a mode of being or a particular quality but in relation to that quality it aims at making me pass from one mode of being to another mode of being. This second mode of being, the ideal of sincerity, I am prevented by nature from attaining, and at the very moment when I struggle to attain it, I have a vague prejudicative comprehension that I shall not attain it. But all the same, in order for me to be able to conceive an intention in bad faith, I must have such a nature that within my being I escape from my being. If I were sad or cowardly in the way in which this inkwell is an inkwell, the possibility of bad faith could not even be conceived. Not only should I be unable to escape from my being; I could not even imagine that I could escape from it. But if bad faith is possible by virtue of a simple project, it is because so far as my being is concerned, there is no differ-

ence between being and non-being if I am cut
off from my project.

Bad faith is possible only because sincerity
is conscious of missing its goal inevitably, due
to its very nature. I can try to apprehend myself as *"not being cowardly,"* when I *am* so,
only on condition that the "being cowardly"
is itself "in question" at the very moment
when it exists, on condition that it is itself *one*
question, that at the very moment when I
wish to apprehend it, it escapes me on all sides
and annihilates itself. The condition under
which I can attempt an effort in bad faith, is
that in one sense, I *am not* this coward which
I do not wish to be. But if I *were not* cowardly
in the simple mode of not-being-what-one-is-
not, I would be "in good faith," by declaring
that I am not cowardly. Thus this inappre-
hensible coward is evanescent; in order for
me not to be cowardly, I must in some way
also be cowardly. That does not mean that I
must be "a little" cowardly, in the sense that
"a little" signifies "to a certain degree cowardly—and not cowardly to a certain degree."
No. I must at once both be and not be totally
and in all aspects a coward. Thus in this case
bad faith requires that I should not be what
I am; that is, that there be an imponderable
difference separating being from non-being
in the mode of being of human reality. But

bad faith is not restricted to denying the qualities which I possess, to not seeing the being which I am. It attempts also to constitute myself as being what I am not. It apprehends me positively as courageous when I am not so. And that is possible, once again, only if I am what I am not; that is, if non-being in me does not have being even by virtue of non-being. Of course necessarily I *am not* courageous; otherwise bad faith would not be *bad* faith. But in addition my effort in bad faith must include the ontological comprehension that even in my usual being what I *am,* I am not it really and that there is no such difference between the being of "being-sad," for example—which I *am* in the mode of not being what I am—and the "non-being" of not-being-courageous which I wish to hide from myself. Moreover it is particularly requisite that the very negation of being should be itself the object of a perpetual annihilation, that the very meaning of "non-being" be perpetually in question in human reality. If I *were not* courageous in the way in which this inkwell is not a table; that is, if I were isolated in my cowardice, propped firmly against it, incapable of putting it in relation to its opposite, if I were not capable of *determining* myself as cowardly—that is, to deny courage to myself and thereby to escape my cowardice in the very moment that I posit it

—if it were not on principle *impossible* for me to coincide with my *not-being-courageous* as well as with my being-courageous— then any project of bad faith would be prohibited me. Thus in order for bad faith to be possible, sincerity itself must be in bad faith. The condition of the possibility for bad faith is that human reality, in its most immediate being, in the inner structure of the prereflective *cogito,* must be what it is not and not be what it is.

III

THE "FAITH" OF BAD FAITH

WE HAVE INDICATED for the moment only those conditions which render bad faith conceivable, the structures of being which permit us to form concepts of bad faith. We can not restrict ourselves to these considerations; we have not yet distinguished bad faith from falsehood. The two-faced concepts which we have described would without a doubt be utilized by a liar to discountenance his questioner, although their two-faced quality being established on the being of man and not on some empirical circumstance, can and ought to be evident to all. The true problem of bad faith stems evidently from the fact that bad faith is *faith*. It can not be either a cynical lie or certainty—if certainty is the intuitive possession of the object. But if we take belief as meaning the adherence of being to its object when the object is not given or is given indistinctly, then bad faith is belief; and the essential problem of bad faith is a prob-

lem of belief. How can we believe by bad
faith in the concepts which we forge ex-
pressly to persuade ourselves? We must note
in fact that the project of bad faith must be
itself in bad faith. I am not only in bad faith
at the end of my effort, when I have con-
structed my two-faced concepts and when I
have persuaded myself. In truth, I have not
persuaded myself; to the extent that I could
be so persuaded, I have always been so.
And at the very moment when I was disposed
to put myself in bad faith, I of necessity was
in bad faith with respect to this same disposition. For me to have represented it to myself
as bad faith would have been cynicism; to believe it sincerely innocent would have been
in good faith. The decision to be in bad faith
does not dare to speak its name; it believes
itself and does not believe itself in bad faith;
it believes itself and does not believe itself
in good faith. It is this which from the
upsurge of bad faith, determines the later attitude and as it were, the *Weltanschauung*
of bad faith.

Bad faith does not hold the norms and cri-
teria of truth as they are accepted by the critical thought of good faith. What it decides
first, in fact, is the nature of truth. With bad
faith a truth appears, a method of thinking, a
type of being which is like that of objects; the
ontological characteristic of the world of bad

faith, with which the subject suddenly surrounds himself, is this *characteristic:* that here being is what it is not, and is not what it is. Consequently a peculiar type of evidence appears; *non-persuasive* evidence. Bad faith apprehends evidence but it is resigned in advance to not being fulfilled by this evidence, to not being persuaded and transformed into good faith. It makes itself humble and modest; it is not ignorant, it says, that faith is decision and that after each intuition, it must decide and *will what it is.* Thus bad faith in its primitive project and in its coming into the world decides on the exact nature of its requirements. It stands forth in the firm resolution *not to demand too much,* to count itself satisfied when it is barely persuaded, to force itself in decisions to adhere to uncertain truths. This original project of bad faith is a decision in bad faith on the nature of faith. Let us understand clearly that there is no question of a reflective, voluntary decision, but of a spontaneous determination of our being. One *puts oneself* in bad faith as one goes to sleep, and one is in bad faith as one dreams. Once this mode of being has been realized, it is as difficult to get out of it as to wake oneself up; bad faith is a type of being in the world, like waking or dreaming, which by itself tends to perpetuate itself, although its structure is of the *metastable* type. But bad faith is conscious of its structure, and it has taken precautions by deciding that the metastable structure is the structure of being and that non-persuasion is the structure of all convictions. It follows that if bad faith is faith and if it includes in its original project its own negation (it determines itself to be not quite convinced in order to convince itself that I am what I am not), then to start with, a faith which wishes itself to be not quite convinced must be possible. What are the conditions for the possibility of such a faith?

I believe that my friend Pierre feels friendship for me. I believe it *in good faith*. I believe it but I do not have for it any self-evident intuition, for the nature of the object does not lend itself to intuition. I *believe it;* that is, I allow myself to give in to all impulses to trust it; I decide to believe in it, and to maintain myself in this decision; I conduct myself, finally, as if I were certain of it, the whole in the synthetic unity of one and the same attitude. This which I define as good faith is what Hegel would call *the immediate.* It is simple faith. Hegel would demonstrate at once that the immediate calls for mediation and that belief by becoming *belief for itself,* passes to the state of non-belief. If I *believe* that my friend Pierre likes me, that means that his friendship appears to me as the meaning of all his acts. Belief is a particular

consciousness *of the meaning* of Pierre's acts.
But if I know that I believe, the belief
appears to me as pure subjective determination without external correlative. This is
what makes the very word "to believe" a term
utilized indifferently to indicate the unwaver-
ing firmness of belief ("My God, I believe in
you") and its character as disarmed and
strictly subjective. ("Is Pierre my friend? I do
not know; I believe so.") But the nature of
consciousness is such that in it the mediate
and the immediate are one and the same
being. To believe is to know that one believes
and to know that one believes is no longer to
believe. Thus to believe is not to believe
any longer because that is only to believe—
this in the unity of one and the same non-
thetic consciousness (of) self. To be sure, we
have here forced the description of the phenomenon by designating it with the word *to
know;* non-thetic consciousness is not to *know.*
But it is in its very translucency at the origin
of all knowing. Thus the non-thetic consciousness (of) believing is destructive of belief. But at the same time the very law of the
prereflective *cogito* implies that the being of
believing ought to be the consciousness of believing.

Thus belief is a being which questions its
own being, which can realize itself only in its
destruction, which can manifest itself to

itself only by denying itself. It is a being for which to be is to appear and to appear is to deny itself. To believe is not to believe. We see the reason for it; the being of consciousness is to exist by itself, then to make itself be and thereby to pass beyond itself. In this sense consciousness is perpetually escaping itself, belief becomes non-belief, the immediate becomes mediation, the absolute becomes relative, and the relative becomes absolute. The ideal of good faith (to believe what one believes) is, like that of sincerity (to be what one is), and ideal of being-in-itself. Every belief is a belief that falls short; one never wholly believes what one believes. Consequently the primitive project of bad faith is only the utilization of this self-destruction through the fact of consciousness. If every belief in good faith is an impossible belief, then there is a place for every impossible belief. My inability to *believe* that I am courageous will not discourage me since every belief involves not quite believing. I shall define this impossible belief as *my* belief. To be sure, I shall not be able to hide from myself that I believe in order not to believe and that I do not believe *in order to* believe. But the subtle, total annihilation of bad faith by itself can not surprise me; it exists at the basis of all faith. What is it then? At the moment when I wish to believe myself courageous I *know* that I am a coward. And this certainly would come to destroy my belief. But *first*, I *am* not any more courageous than cowardly, if we are to understand this in the mode of being of the in-itself. In the second place, I do not *know* that I am courageous; such a view of myself can be accompanied only by *belief*, for it surpasses pure reflective certitude. In the third place, it is very true that bad faith does not succeed in believing what it wishes to believe. But it is precisely as the acceptance of not believing what it believes that it is bad faith. Good faith wishes to flee the "not-believing-what-one-believes" by finding refuge in being. Bad faith flees being by taking refuge in "not-believing-what-one-believes." It has disarmed all beliefs in advance—those which it would like to take hold of and, by the same stroke, the others, those which it wishes to flee. In *willing* this self-destruction of belief, from which science escapes by searching for evidence, it ruins the beliefs which are opposed to it, which reveal themselves as *being only belief*. Thus we can better understand the original phenomenon of bad faith.

In bad faith there is no cynical lie, nor knowing preparation for deceitful concepts. But the first act of bad faith is to flee what it can not flee, to flee what it is. The very project of flight reveals to bad faith an inner disintegration in the heart of being, and it is this disintegration which it wishes to be. In truth, the two immediate attitudes which we can take in the face of our being are conditioned by the very nature of this being and its immediate relation with the in-itself. Good faith seeks to flee the inner disintegration of my being in the direction of the in-itself which it should be and is not. Bad faith seeks to flee the in-itself by means of the inner disintegration of my being. But it denies this very disintegration as it denies that it is itself bad faith. Bad faith seeks by means of "not-being-what-one-is" to escape from the in-itself which I am not in the mode of being what one is not. It denies itself as bad faith and aims at the in-itself which I am not in the mode of "not-being-what-one-is-not."[1] If bad faith is possible, it is because it is an immediate, permanent threat to every project of the human being; it is because consciousness conceals in its being a permanent risk of bad faith. The origin of this risk is that the nature of consciousness simultaneously is to be what it is not and not to be what it is. In the

---

[1] If it is indifferent whether one is in good or in bad faith, because bad faith reapprehends good faith and slides to the very origin of the project of good faith, that does not mean that we can not radically escape bad faith. But that supposes a self-recovery of being which was previously corrupted. This self-recovery we shall call authenticity, the description of which has no place here.

light of these remarks we can now approach the ontological study of consciousness, not as the totality of the human being, but as the instantaneous nucleus of this being.